Careers in Focus

Entrepreneurs

Ferguson Publishing Company
Chicago, Illinois

Copyright © 1999 Ferguson Publishing Company
ISBN 0-89434-284-3

Library of Congress Cataloging-in-Publication Data

Careers in focus.   Entrepreneurs.
        p.   cm.
    Includes index.
    Summary: An overview of entrepreneurship and descriptions of twenty-one
fast-growing careers in the field including information on each about requirements, work environment, earnings, and outlook.
        ISBN 0-89434-284-3
        1. Vocational guidance—Juvenile literature.   2. Entrepreneurship—
Vocational guidance—Juvenile literature. [1. Entrepreneurship—Vocational
guidance. 2. Vocational guidance.] I. Title: Entrepreneurs.
HF5381.2.C376   1999
331.7′02--dc21   99-33444
                                               CIP

Printed in the United States of America

Cover photo courtesy The Stock Market

Published and distributed by
Ferguson Publishing Company
200 West Jackson, 7th Floor
Chicago, Illinois 60606
312-692-1000

W-8

Table of Contents

Introduction

Entrepreneurs are people who set up and manage their own business enterprises—assuming the risks if they fail, reaping the rewards if they succeed. Owning a small business has been part of the American dream since the earliest days of the country, and the late 20th century saw a great increase in entrepreneurial ambition. This may be in part due to the downsizing trends of American companies. Whereas earlier in the century, a person could work for one company until retirement, such job security has become more rare. It's increasingly common for men and women in their 50s to lose their jobs, and find themselves with few job prospects. With severance pay in hand, these people often invest in the businesses they've been longing for, recognizing these ventures as no more risky than any other career pursuit. Once upon a time, a person chose a job path and stuck with it; these days, people experiment with a variety of careers throughout their lives.

There are over 400 colleges and universities that offer entrepreneurship courses—200 more than there were in 1984. There are also more organizations, periodicals, and Web pages advising people on how to start their own businesses and keep them running. *Entrepreneur* and *Success* magazines publish special issues devoted to small business and maintain Web sites. The Small Business Administration (SBA) guarantees more than $10 billion in loans every year; 24 percent of the loans from the SBA's largest program go to minority-owned businesses. The SBA also provides business start-up kits, workshops, and research assistance.

Despite some discouraging statistics that put small business failure at 50 percent, the number of entrepreneurial ventures will only increase. The majority of business school graduates will make their careers with entrepreneurships, either by starting their own businesses or by hiring on with small business owners. With a number of professional organizations and the SBA devoted to small business, the new entrepreneur can find a great deal of support—technical, financial, and emotional. Home-based businesses in particular are growing at a rapid rate, aided in part by the Internet. It's estimated that 20 percent of all small businesses are home-based.

Not only has the Internet allowed entrepreneurs to promote their businesses internationally, but it has provided great new job prospects including Web design, online consulting, online research, and Web mastering (maintaining and updating business Web sites). As the Internet expands and develops, more people will peddle their own wares and talents online. But the Internet isn't the only opportunity for new entrepreneurships; new trends and habits are what have inspired such enterprises as personal cheffing, medical billing, and personal training.

Faced with corporate downsizing in the 1990s, more people began to examine their roles in the workplace. Today, people don't just want jobs—they want fulfilling careers, rewarding both financially and emotionally. They also want time for the other aspects of their lives, such as families, hobbies, and traveling. The ideal home-based business can offer these things, but not all small business endeavors turn out as planned. While some would-be entrepreneurs with failed businesses return to the corporate world, others try again with different entrepreneurships.

Each article in this book discusses a particular arts and entertainment occupation in detail. The information comes from Ferguson's *Encyclopedia of Careers and Vocational Guidance.* The History section describes the history of the particular job as it relates to the overall development of its industry or field. The Job describes the primary and secondary duties of the job. Requirements discusses high school and postsecondary education and training requirements, any certification or licensing necessary, and any other personal requirements for success in the job. Exploring offers suggestions on how to gain some experience in or knowledge of the particular job before making a firm educational and financial commitment. The focus is on what can be done while still in high school (or in the early years of college) to gain a better understanding of the job. The Employers section gives an overview of typical places of employment for the job. Starting Out discusses the best ways to land that first job, be it through the college placement office, newspaper ads, or personal contact. The Advancement section describes what kind of career path to expect from the job and how to get there. Earnings lists salary ranges and describes the typical fringe benefits. The Work Environment section describes the typical surroundings and conditions of employment—whether indoors or outdoors, noisy or quiet, social or independent, and so on. Also discussed are typical hours worked, any seasonal fluctuations, and the stresses and strains of the job. The Outlook section summarizes the job in terms of the general economy and industry projections. For the most part, Outlook information is obtained from the Bureau of Labor Statistics and is supplemented by information taken from professional associations. Job growth terms follow those used in the *Occupational Outlook Handbook:* Growth described as "much faster than the average" means an increase of 36 percent or more. Growth described as "faster than the average" means an increase of 21 to 35 percent. Growth described as "about as fast as the average" means an increase of 10 to 20 percent. Growth described as "little change or more slowly than the average" means an increase of 0 to 9 percent. "Decline" means a decrease of 1 percent or more.

Each article ends with For More Information, which lists organizations that can provide career information on training, education, internships, scholarships, and job placement.

Adult Day Care Coordinators

	School Subjects
Business Psychology Sociology	
	Personal Skills
Helping/teaching Leadership/management	
	Work Environment
Primarily indoors Primarily one location	
	Minimum Education Level
Associate's degree	
	Salary Range
$15,000 to $35,000 to $75,000	
	Certification or Licensing
Required for certain positions	
	Outlook
Much faster than the average	

Overview

Adult day care coordinators direct day care programs for adults—usually elderly or disabled—who cannot be left alone all day. They oversee staff members who provide care, meals, and social activities to day care clients and serve as a liaison between the day care center and its clients' families. There are more than 4,000 adult day services in the country.

History

Adult day care had its beginnings in the 1940s in psychiatric hospitals. It started as an effort to help patients who had been released from mental institutions. Over the next 20 years the focus gradually shifted from psychiatric care to other kinds of health maintenance. The landmark publication,

Developing Day Care for Older People, published by the National Council on Aging (NCOA) in 1972, provided technical assistance for establishing adult day care, and by 1978 there were nearly 300 adult day care centers throughout the United States.

In the 1980s the first Congressional hearing was held on adult day care programs and the Economic Recovery Act was passed, allowing a tax credit to families with elderly members in day care. NCOA established voluntary standards.

There are now more than 4,000 adult day centers currently operating in the United States. Approximately 90 percent operate on a nonprofit or public basis and many are affiliated with larger organizations such as home care, skilled nursing facilities, medical centers, or multipurpose senior organizations.

The Job

If you have grandparents or other relatives dealing with the challenges of growing old, then you know how much assistance they need just to perform many of the routines you may take for granted. Many of the people who go into adult day service do so because they want to help older adults, and adults with disabilities, to continue to live with their families. An adult day service is open during regular working hours, typically from 8 AM to 6 PM Monday through Friday, allowing those family members who care for adults to go to work during the day. Some adult day services have transportation that pick up the elderly and other adults, then drop them back at their homes. These services are gaining in popularity because they cost much less than nursing homes, and offer more personal care.

Amy Pantages owns Seniors Are Us, an adult day service in Ormond Beach, Florida. The facility consists of eight rooms, which includes two lounges, an exercise room, beauty shop, and nurse's office. Though she has a staff which includes aides and an activities director, Amy is directly involved in the care giving. "We take care of people who've had strokes, have Alzheimer's, diabetes," she says. "If family members work, it's wonderful for them. It's an alternative to a nursing home, or assisted living." The service also has a nurse to administer medication and check vital signs, as well as a doctor on call.

Your duties as the owner and coordinator of an adult day service will vary depending upon the size of the center and the services it offers. Your general responsibility is to ensure that your center provides the necessary care for its clients. This may include personal hygiene, meals, medications and therapies, and social activities.

Though you may choose to be involved in the daily care of your clients, you may also choose to focus on administrative concerns. In either case, you'll oversee various staff members who provide the care giving. A large center, for example, might have a nurse, a physical therapist, a social worker, a cook, and several aides. You're responsible for staff hiring, training, and scheduling. You may meet with staff members either one-on-one or in group sessions to review and discuss plans for the clients.

Overseeing meal planning and preparation is also your responsibility. In most centers, clients are given a noon meal, and usually juices and snacks in the mornings and afternoons. You'll work with a cook or dietitian to develop well-rounded menus that take into account the nutritional needs of the clients, including any particular restrictions such as a diabetic or low-sodium diet. You may also oversee the purchasing and inventory of the center's food supply.

You'll schedule daily and weekly activities for the day care clients. Depending upon the particular needs and abilities of the clients, a recreational schedule might include crafts, games, exercises, reading time, or movies. In some centers, clients are taken on outings to shopping centers, parks, or restaurants. You'll plan such outings, arranging for transportation and any reservations or special accommodations that are necessary. You'll also organize parties for special events, such as holidays or birthdays.

"I do all the cooking," Amy says. "They all come in at one time—20 people on 2 buses. We try to get them rolling with breakfast; we read the paper to them every morning, do the crossword puzzle." The day includes an exercise program, non-denominational devotional, group games, and outings. "I only take people who can maintain a structured day," she says, "so when we're doing an activity, no one will start screaming. We do change diapers and help feed people, but if they can't move on their own, I won't take them. I don't have the facilities for it, and I don't want my staff to get hurt." Alzheimer's patients often require special attention. In the afternoons, these clients often become restless and unfocused. "We'll work with them one-on-one to get them to settle down," she says. "We'll give them manicures, let them listen to Walkmans."

In addition to planning and overseeing the activities of the center and its clients, you'll work closely with client family members to make sure that each individual is receiving care that best fits his or her needs. This relationship with the clients' families usually begins before the client is ever actually placed in the day care center.

When a new family is considering placing an elderly person in a day care setting, they often have many questions about the center and its activities. You'll meet with family members to show them the center and explain to them how it is run. You'll also gather information about the potential client, including names and phone numbers of doctors and people to contact in cases of emergency; lists of medications taken with instructions on when and how they should be administered; and information on allergies, food choices, and daily habits and routines.

After the client is placed in the center, you may meet periodically with his or her family to update them on how the client is responding to the day care setting. If necessary, you may advise the family about social services, such as home health care, and refer them to other providers.

You'll also oversee the business and administrative details of the service, developing and adhering to a budget for the center. If the center is licensed or certified by the state, you may ensure that it remains in compliance with the regulations and necessary documentation. You'll also be responsible for general bookkeeping, bill payment, and office management.

Requirements

High School

Although the vast majority of employers require at least a high school diploma, there are no definite educational requirements for becoming an adult day care coordinator. Some people learn their skills on the job; others have taken college courses in home nursing or health care. History, social studies, and sociology courses will help you prepare for a college program in social work. Take courses in business and accounting to prepare for the administrative details of running an adult day service. English and composition courses will help you develop the writing skills necessary for preparing grant applications and other reports, and will also help you to develop communication skills needed for working with clients and their families.

Postsecondary Training

Many employers prefer to hire candidates who meet the standards set by the National Adult Day Services Association. In order to meet these standards, a coordinator must have a bachelor's degree in health or social services or a related field, with one year's supervisory experience in a social or health services setting. In preparation for such a career, a college student might choose occupational, recreational, or rehabilitation therapy or social work. An increasingly popular major for potential adult day care coordinators is gerontology, or geriatrics.

More than 600 colleges and universities in the United States offer a formal program of instruction in gerontology. Although specific courses vary from school to school, most programs consist of classes in social gerontology, biology and physiology of aging, psychology of aging, and sociology of aging. In addition to these 4 core classes, most programs offer elective courses in such areas as social policy, community services, nutrition and exercise, diversity in aging, health issues, death and dying, and ethics and life extension.

A practicum or field placement is also a part of most gerontology programs. This allows students to obtain experience working with both well-functioning elderly people and those with age-related disabilities.

Certification or Licensing

No certification or licensing is required to become an adult day care coordinator. Your state may require that you license your service with the state health department, or some other health care agency. The kind of funding you receive will also determine licensing requirements; any adult day care center that receives payment from Medicare or from other government agencies must be certified by the state's department of health. The standards set by NADSA are voluntary; new accreditation processes are in development. NADSA does offer certification for program assistants, administrators, and directors.

Other Requirements

Compassion and an affinity for the elderly and disabled are vital, as are patience and the desire to help others. Amy credits her success to her nine years of nursing home experience and her genuine interest in the well-being of her clients. "I truly love what I do," she says. "I care about these people." By being directly involved in the care giving, she has earned the respect of her staff which helps her to maintain workers in a field with a high burn-out factor. She also pays her staff well in order to keep them with the service. Amy also takes an interest in her clients, listening to them and giving them her attention. "They talk about stuff they would never talk to their kids about," she says. "They also have great histories."

Exploring

The easiest way to learn about elder care is to visit a nursing home or adult day care center in order to experience firsthand what it is like to interact with elderly people. You could even take a volunteer position or part-time job in such a facility. A local social services agency may also have volunteer and part-time opportunities; these services often need people to read to the elderly and the blind, to clean the homes of the elderly and those with disabilities, and to run errands. Many agencies and churches also sponsor "Adopt-A-Grandparent" programs which would allow you to serve as a "companion" to an elderly person, visiting him or her a few times a week for conversation and friendship.

You might also check your local library for books or articles on aging in order to learn more about this career.

Employers

NADSA estimates that 90 percent of the adult day services in the country are operated on a nonprofit or public basis. Adult day services are often part of home care organizations, health centers, and senior organizations. But the great demand for adult day services, and the fact that more insurance companies are beginning to cover day care fees, are leading more people to start their own facilities. Franchise opportunities exist with such companies as Home Instead Senior Care.

Starting Out

Before investing in your own business, you'll need some experience in elder care. Your college program should be able to direct you to job opportunities in social services and geriatrics. Often jobs with nursing homes and social service agencies are listed in the classifieds of the local newspaper. You can also contact organizations directly. Another means of finding job leads is to become affiliated with a professional association, such as the American Geriatrics Society and the American Association of Home and Services for the Aging. Many such organizations have monthly or quarterly newsletters that list job opportunities. Some also have job banks and referral services.

After gaining experience in elder care, you'll have some understanding of the requirements of an adult day service, and an understanding of funding options and organizations. NADSA can provide you with their standards and guidelines for adult day services. You can also contact an adult day service franchiser for more information about starting a business.

Advancement

When you've established one facility, you may choose to open other facilities in different areas of your community, or in nearby towns. You may also choose to expand the services of your center, such as arranging for specialists to be on call. Some successful centers expand their hours to include weekends, or 24-hour care. As an experienced adult day service coordinator, you may decide to share your knowledge by speaking to organizations, serving on the boards of regional and national associations, and writing articles for publication.

Finally, you might choose to return to school and complete a higher degree—often a master's degree in social work. If you choose this option, there are many career opportunities in the field of social services. *Social workers* might, for example, work with individuals and families dealing with AIDS, cancer, or other debilitating illnesses. They might also work for agencies offering various types of counseling, rehabilitation, or crisis intervention.

Earnings

Funding for adult day services comes from private pay (participant fees), insurance companies, managed care organizations, government programs, grants, and other sources. NADSA estimates daily fees to run from several dollars to $185 per participant. According to the Dementia Services Program, the total expenses for an adult day center are around $250,000 a year (including administrative salaries), and the total revenue around $265,000 a year. This leaves $15,000 surplus to put back into the business. Total administrative staff expenses (which would include your salary) are estimated at $42,500.

According to the Association for Gerontology in Higher Education, beginning annual salaries range from $18,000 to $31,000 for persons with a bachelor's degree and little experience. Generally, coordinators who do not have a bachelor's degree can expect to earn somewhat less than this. Experienced coordinators with a bachelor's degree employed in large, well-funded centers may earn from $20,000 to $45,000 annually.

As the coordinator and owner of an adult day service, you'll provide your staff with fringe benefits. These benefits would include a group health plan of which you could be a part.

Work Environment

Most adult day care centers have a schedule that corresponds to standard business hours. You'll likely work a 40 to 50 hour week, Monday through Friday with weekends off.

Your work environment will vary depending upon the size and type of center. Some centers are fairly institutional, resembling children's day care centers or nursing homes. Others have a more residential-feel, carpeted and furnished like a private home. Regardless of the furnishings, the center is typically clean, well-lit, and equipped with ramps, rails, and other devices that ensure the safety of clients.

Part of your day may be spent in the center's common areas with clients and staff. You may also spend time working in an on-site office. If the staff members take clients on outings, you may accompany them.

You'll be on your feet much of the time, ensuring that meals and activities run smoothly, and helping staff members when necessary.

Regardless of the size of the center, you'll spend the majority of your time working with people—staff members and day care clients. Working with clients is often very trying. Many of them may have had a stroke or have Alzheimer's disease, and may be confused, uncooperative, and even hostile. The job may also be emotionally taxing for the coordinator who becomes attached to his or her clients. Most adults who use a day care center are elderly or permanently disabled; for this reason, day care staff must frequently deal with the decline and eventual death of their clients.

Outlook

NADSA reports that 14 million people will need elder care within the next 20 years. Insurance companies are recognizing day centers as less expensive alternatives to long-term care, and are beginning to provide coverage for day services. To meet the demand for services, long term facilities will expand to include day care, and more individuals with elder care experience will invest in their own centers. Look for more rigid national standards to develop in order to help people find quality senior care.

New sources of training are also in development. Those interested in starting adult day services will benefit from training sessions, conferences, and teaching centers offered by national organizations and state associations. Partners in Caregiving: The Adult Day Services Program is a new national assistance program in development. As part of the Wake Forest University School of Medicine, the program will sponsor education opportunities, telephone assistance, online services, and a national publication for the owners of adult day services.

For More Information

To learn about job opportunities, issues affecting adult day services, and membership information, contact:

American Association of Homes and Services for the Aging
901 E Street, NW, Suite 500
Washington, DC 20004-2011
Tel: 202-783-2242
Web: http://www.aahsa.org

To learn about certification, national standards, and current issues in adult day service, contact:

National Adult Day Services Association
National Council on Aging
409 Third Street, SW, Suite 200
Washington, DC 20024
Tel: 202-479-6682
Email: nadsa@ncoa.org
Web: http://www.ncoa.org/nadsa

The following organizations offer information on aging, services for the elderly, and careers in gerontology.

American Geriatrics Society
770 Lexington Avenue, Suite 300
New York, NY 10021
Tel: 212-308-1414
Email: info.arnger@americangeriatrics.org
Web: http://www.americangeriatrics.org

Association for Gerontology in Higher Education
1030 15th Street, NW, Suite 240
Washington, DC 20005-1503
Tel: 202-289-9806
Email: aghetemp@aghe.org
Web: http://www.aghe.org

Gerontological Society of America
1030 15th Street, NW, Suite 250
Washington, DC 20005-1503
Tel: 202-842-1275
Web: http://www.geron.org

National Association of Area Agencies on Aging
927 15th Street, NW, Sixth Floor
Washington, DC 20005
Tel: 202-296-8130
Web: http://www.n4a.org

Automobile Detailing Service Owners

School Subjects
Chemistry
Technical/Shop

Personal Skills
Mechanical/manipulative

Work Environment
Primarily multiple locations
Primarily outdoors

Minimum Education Level
Some postsecondary training

Salary Range
$18,000 to $45,000 to $100,000+

Certification or Licensing
None available

Outlook
Faster than the average

Overview

Automobile detailing is the careful cleaning of the interiors and exteriors of cars, vans, boats, and other vehicles. People use the services of a detailing business to keep their vehicles looking new. The owner of a detailing service will either detail in a commercial shop, or will visit the client's home with a specially equipped van. There are approximately 12,000 detail businesses in the automotive "appearance-care" industry. *Automobile detailers* work all across the United States, but find the work to be most steady in states where the weather is mild year-round.

History

In the years before World War I, there were fewer than a million cars on the roads and streets of the United States; in the years after, the number grew to five million. By 1925, there were 20 million cars in the nation. About this time, industry pioneer Henry Ford (1863-1947) quit producing the Model T because of the growth of the used-car market. People could buy better-quality used cars for the same price as the mass-produced Model T. Other car companies met the challenge of the used-car market by developing a new version of a familiar model every year.

The used-car market, along with the evolution of cars as status symbols, contributed to the development of the car appearance industry. Auto-detailers were first hired by used-car dealers to prepare damaged cars for resale. The late 1940s saw the introduction of Turtle Wax (then known as Plastone) and other car-care products, as well as the first automatic car washes. The average lifespan of a car in 1971 was a little over five years; now cars last nearly eight. Auto detailers and car-care products help keep these longer-lasting cars looking new.

The Job

As with other cleaning services, auto detailing is great work for the clean "freak." And if you happen to be a car lover, too, then you're in business! With some training, a specially equipped van, and a good eye for detail, you can get old cars looking new again and keep new cars looking new. In some cases, you'll just do a basic wash and vacuum, but in other cases you'll focus on cleaning every nook and cranny of a car, inside and out. You'll polish and wax the exterior surface, clean and protect any rubber, trim, glass, and chrome. You'll clean the wheels and tires. Inside the car, you'll vacuum the carpet, treat the vinyl and leather, and clean the dash and vents. You'll attend to stubborn stains like road tar, tree sap, and grease. With the proper equipment, you can sand and buff exterior paint jobs. A detailer must have an understanding of cleaners and how they work, and must be creative in dealing with troublesome blotches and blemishes. Though you'll rely on specially formulated cleaners, you'll also find some household items useful in getting at stubborn interior stains, items like vinegar (for all-purpose cleaning), cornstarch (for grease and oil), and pencil erasers (for ink and crayon marks).

"Mobile" detailing is when you offer services to clients at their homes or office parking lots. Many people prefer the services of a mobile detailing service; having the service come to them eliminates the need for driving to a commercial service, and waiting for the car to be cleaned. With a mobile detailing service, you can also service corporate fleets of vans, trucks, and even light aircraft.

Anthony Rabak owns a mobile detailing service that serves the areas of Elk Grove, Laguna, and Sacramento, California. With a special cargo van equipped with its own water and power supply, Anthony takes to the streets to attend to his appointments. "I'm the kind of person who pays attention to the little things," Anthony says, "which is very important in detailing. Don't cut corners!" To assure that he blasts every speck of dirt and grime, Anthony carries 110 gallons of purified water in his van, along with an electric pressure washer, a 50-foot hose, and a short-nozzle spray gun. "I use purified water because it doesn't leave water spots," he says. "And I chose an electric washer because they are much quieter in a residential area and you can usually plug them into a power source at a location." In case there isn't a power source on site, Anthony has a gas-powered generator and a power inverter.

"Usually I perform most of my work in the shade," Anthony says, "and when there isn't any I make my own with a portable, folding canopy tent." His time on site varies according to how much detailing the vehicle owner requests. A basic car wash takes about an hour, while a full detail can take all day. In addition to the power washer and hose, Anthony uses a simple bucket, car wash soap, and natural sea sponges on the cars' exteriors. "I use the sea sponges," he says, "because they cause the least amount of scratches." He also uses towels, special cleaning brushes, and a variety of cleaning chemicals. With a speed rotary polisher, and a dual head orbital polisher, Anthony can effectively wax paint and scrub carpets. "I also use a shop vacuum with a specially made 15-foot hose and various attachments," Anthony says. For stubborn carpet and upholstery stains, Anthony uses a shampoo machine, but often times just uses a spray shampoo, scrub brush, and elbow grease.

Some detailers specialize in exotic cars, like Porsches, Jaguars, or Lamborghinis, preparing the cars for shows, races, and other events, while others will clean anything from an RV to a golf cart. As a detailer, you may set up special maintenance contracts with individuals or businesses, regularly servicing vehicles every six or eight weeks. Most individual clients, however, only request detailing services once or twice a year. Those detailers who own their own shops may offer more than cleaning. With a garage and employees, a detailer can offer painting, windshield repair, dent removal, leather dying, and other interior and exterior improvements.

Requirements

High School

Take courses that will prepare you for small business ownership. Math and accounting courses will help prepare you for the bookkeeping tasks of the work. You should also take any other business or economic courses that will give you some insight into the market place and the requirements of running a profitable business. Join your high school's business club to learn about business practices, and to meet local entrepreneurs. English courses can help you develop communication skills for dealing with clients and promoting your service. Chemistry and technical/shop courses will give you an understanding of the cleansers and equipment you'll be using.

Postsecondary Training

Though a college degree isn't required to be a detailer, courses in small business management from a community college can give you insight into building a successful service. Work with a detailer to learn the business; check with a local detailing chain, or local garage for training. Some companies offer detailing training, such as franchisers Maaco, Ziebart, or National Detail.

Certification or Licensing

A business license may be required by your city; some cities and states also require special licenses for mobile service work. You won't need to be certified, but many detailers are concerned about the lack of standardization within the industry. A survey by *Professional Carwashing and Detailing* magazine found that 84 percent of the respondents have had to fix finishes harmed by another detailer. Whether any kind of regulation comes in the future depends on the International Carwash Association (ICA) which took over the Professional Detailing Association in 1997.

Other Requirements

Because it's fairly inexpensive to purchase the equipment for a mobile detailing service, it's important for you to be very professional and dedicated to the customer. Any bad word of mouth can hurt your business, sending potential customers to one of your many competitors. "People are comfortable when you arrive in a clean, organized service vehicle," Anthony says. He also wears a uniform, and is always polite to his clients. "I show that I have an interest in them as a person, and not just their car. People like to have a relationship with people who provide services for them."

As with any small business, you're entirely responsible for your own success. You must be ambitious and self-motivated. You won't have anyone scheduling your work hours for you, so you must be disciplined. You must also be capable of budgeting your money for the months when business may be slow.

Exploring

Cleaning a car well requires more than a hose and a bucket; but even without all the proper equipment, you can learn much about cleansers and their effect on a car's exterior simply by washing the family vehicle. Learn on your own how to clean a windshield without leaving streaks, and how to best remove stains from interior carpets and upholstery. Anthony explored the job through research. "I read every book on automobile detailing I could find at the library and bookstores," he says. "I talked with detailing supply distributors." Spend a few days with a local detailer with a good reputation to get a sense of the job. Interview detailers in your area to find out what equipment they use, how much they charge, and how many hours they work. Professional Carwashing and Detailing Online (http://www.carwash.com) features many articles on the business, as well as a bulletin board for industry professionals.

Employers

A number of companies that sell supplies and equipment also offer franchise opportunities. By franchising with a detail chain like Ziebart or National Detail, you'll receive discounts, phone support, and marketing assistance.

But be very careful selecting a company to work with; some operations sell equipment at a very large price and offer very little support. Check with ICA, or consult *Professional Carwashing and Detailing* magazine for reputable companies.

Starting Out

The books on detailing you've read, and the other research you've conducted, should give you an idea of the equipment you'll be needing. Before buying, be sure to price-shop the supply and equipment distributors for the best deals. Starting out, you'll need about $500 to pay for an electric buffer, a shop vacuum, and for the polishes, waxes, and other cleaning chemicals. Due to the high cost of water tanks, Anthony rents one.

It took a while for Anthony to get his business going. He tried traditional advertising, including a listing in the Yellow Pages, but none of it produced much interest. But eventually word got around that he did good work, and business picked up. "The best results," he says, "have come from word-of-mouth—people who were happy with my work, showed their cars to others, and highly recommended me."

Advancement

Once your business has taken off, you may feel the need to hire employees and purchase more vans to serve more customers. Some detailing services contract with utility companies, police departments, car dealerships, and other clients with large numbers of vehicles to clean regularly. You may also choose to open your own shop and expand the number of services offered. Many detailing services offer painting and minor collision repair. They may also do special pin-striping, upholstery repair, and convertible top replacement.

Earnings

The revenue for an automobile detailing establishment depends on the size of the business, the operating costs, the number of employees, location, years in the business, and many other factors. Obviously, a single-operator mobile detailing service won't have as many customers as a large, multiple-bay car wash/detailing business. A mobile detailer will make anywhere from $30 to $60 per hour, charging between $25 and $40 for a basic detail, depending on the size of the vehicle. A complete detail can cost between $60 and $300, depending on the condition of the vehicle.

Based on figures compiled for the 1998 detailing survey by *Professional Carwashing and Detailing* magazine, the average freestanding shop makes approximately $93,000 a year, after subtracting operating expenses. (According to the survey, average annual operating expenses are $63,200 per shop, which includes the cost of equipment and supplies, chemicals, employee wages, rent, utilities, and advertising.) The average mobile detailing service grosses about $41,000, and has considerably lower operating expenses.

Work Environment

You'll be working mostly on your own, without much supervision. Your work, however, will be carefully scrutinized by your customers who are expecting their cars to shine like new. "It's a great feeling when you see how pleased and amazed people are with your work," Anthony says. The work can be physically demanding, requiring some crawling around and bending; you also spend a lot of time on your feet. In some cases, you'll be using harsh chemicals which may irritate your skin and any allergies. Most of your work will be outside, unless you own a shop where some services will be performed in the garage. Therefore, weather conditions greatly affect your work.

Anthony charges by the hour, but there are many hours for which he isn't paid: driving to and from an appointment, bookkeeping, scheduling services. "You're responsible for all aspects of your business," Anthony says. "You are the public relations person, the advertiser, the receptionist/secretary/file clerk, etc." You can, however, set your own hours, scheduling appointments only for those days you choose. But you'll also have to work as regularly as possible during the spring and summer months if living in an area with cold winters.

Outlook

Some auto industry experts predict that the year 2030 will see a billion cars on the streets of the world. And car owners will be using their cars as offices, making phone calls, faxing information, and working from a computer, to take advantage of every available minute. With more time spent in their cars, people will take better care of them, calling in the services of automobile detailers. Cars are also built to last longer these days, and the prices are always rising; therefore, people will be hiring detailers to help them keep their older cars looking nice. The mobile detailer will especially benefit from the longer working hours of double-income couples; people will prefer detailing services to come to them, rather than take the time to drive to a service and sit in line.

A detailer will have to keep up-to-date on the latest cleansers and treatments as cars suffer more damage from acid rain and from the chemicals used to clean and clear streets. It's uncertain yet, however, how much detailers will be able to rely on each other to create a professional entity. Some believe the closing of the Professional Detailing Association was a sign of a lack of unity among detailers. But the ICA, a much larger organization, is dedicated to serving both car wash operators and detailers alike.

For More Information

To learn more about the current issues affecting car washing and detailing, visit Professional Carwashing and Detailing Online, or write to the address below for subscription information:

Professional Carwashing and Detailing
National Trade Publications, Inc.
13 Century Hill Drive
Latham, NY 12110
Tel: 518-783-1281
Web: http://carwash.com/

Bed and Breakfast Owners

School Subjects
Business
Family and consumer science

Personal Skills
Communication/ideas
Leadership/management

Work Environment
Primarily one location
Indoors and outdoors

Minimum Education Level
High school diploma

Salary Range
$7,000 to $75,000 to $140,000+

Certification or Licensing
Required by certain states

Outlook
About as fast as the average

Overview

A bed and breakfast is an inn, or small hotel, of about 4 to 20 rooms. The owner of the bed and breakfast, either single-handedly or with the help of spouse and family, provides guests with a comfortable, home-like environment. *Bed and breakfast owners,* sometimes called *innkeepers,* clean rooms, assign rooms to guests, keep books and records, and provide some meals. They also actively interact with guests and provide information about tours, museums, restaurants, theaters, and recreational areas. There are between 15,000 and 20,000 bed and breakfasts in the country. Though a bed and breakfast may be located in the very heart of a large city, most are located in small towns, the country, and along oceans, lakes, or rivers.

History

"There was no room in the inn"—it's a line that's been used for years in Christmas pageants, conjuring up the image of cranky innkeepers mean enough to turn away a pregnant woman in the dark of night. But Mary and Joseph didn't likely miss out on much by staying in a stable—the inns of their day were very primitive, stone structures that provided little more than a roof overhead.

So how did the lodging industry move from these stark offerings to the grand excess of something like Caesar's Palace in Las Vegas with its talking statues, moving sidewalks, and private jacuzzis? And how do you explain the funky "motor hotels" of the 1950s—with cottages shaped like wigwams that contained vibrating beds? And where does the bed and breakfast fit in? Actually, the "b & b," as it's affectionately known, is an example of some of the most basic and traditional forms of lodging, along with some very comfortable and charming frills. Though initially considered nothing more than a bed for weary travelers, inns became, over the centuries, clean and comfortable establishments that provided good rest and good food and served as important community centers. Some of the first Elizabethan theaters were simply the courtyards of English lodges. The lodging houses of the first American colonies were styled after these English inns and were considered so necessary that a law in 18th-century Massachusetts required that towns provide roadside lodging.

These early examples of bed and breakfasts thrived for years, until the development of the railroad. Large luxury hotels popped up next to railroad stations and did a booming business. Some inns survived, but many became more like hotels in the process, adding rooms and giving less personal service. Other inns became boarding houses, renting rooms by the week and the month. When people took to the highways in automobiles, lodging changed once again, inspiring the development of motels and tourist camps. It has only been in the last 20 years or so that inns have become popular forms of lodging again, with bed and breakfasts opening up in historic houses and towns. In 1980, there were approximately 5,000 inns in the country; today, that number has nearly quadrupled.

The Job

Have you ever wanted to vacation with FBI's Public Enemy #1? Probably not. But in Tucson, Arizona, you can sit in the jacuzzi of the Dillinger House Bed and Breakfast and imagine yourself the pampered 1930s-era bank robber John Dillinger. Mark Muchmore now owns the house and grounds where Dillinger was captured. Though a house with such history may not seem a natural source for a bed and breakfast, the history actually gives the place a unique distinction in the area. Dillinger's respite in the desert town is part of local legend, and his capture is still celebrated with annual parties and dramatic re-creations in some of Tucson's bars. One of the great appeals of bed and breakfasts are the stories behind them. Though not every bed and breakfast has a history as colorful as that of the Dillinger House, many do have well-documented backgrounds. Bed and breakfast owners therefore become great sources of local history and valuable guides to area sites.

Most of the bed and breakfasts across the country are housed in historical structures: the Victorian houses of Cape May, New Jersey; Brooklyn brownstones; a house in Illinois designed by Frank Lloyd Wright. And many are furnished with antiques. Mark owned his house for some time before turning it into a bed and breakfast. A job change inspired him to start a new business, opening up his home to guests. "I had always wanted to do something like this," he says. "I already had the property, a large house, and two adjacent guest houses, so it seemed perfect."

As the name "bed and breakfast" suggests, a good home-made breakfast is an essential part of any inn stay. Mark's day starts much earlier than Dillinger's ever did and is likely much more serene; he's typically up at 5:00 AM grinding coffee beans, harvesting herbs, and preparing to bake. "I accommodate any and all dietary restrictions," Mark says, "and do it in such a way that my guests feel really paid attention to and respected." After serving his guests their breakfast and cleaning up, Mark sees to business concerns such as answering email messages, calling prospective guests, and taking reservations. Once the guests have left their rooms, Mark can clean the rooms and do some laundry. After grocery shopping, Mark returns to his office for book work and to prepare brochures for the mail.

Among all the daily tasks, Mark reserves time to get to know his guests and to make sure they're enjoying their stay. "I like interacting with my guests," he says. "I like hearing about their jobs, their lives, their likes and dislikes. I love to be able to give them sight-seeing suggestions, restaurant tips, and from time to time, little extras like a bowl of fresh citrus from my trees." It is such close attention to detail that makes a bed and breakfast successful. The guests of bed and breakfasts are looking for more personal attention and warmer hospitality than they'd receive from a large hotel chain.

Though the owners of bed and breakfasts are giving up much of their privacy by allowing guests to stay in the rooms of their own homes, they do have their houses to themselves from time to time. Some bed and breakfasts are only open during peak tourist season, and some are only open on weekends. And even those open year-round may often be without guests. For some owners, inconsistency in the business is not a problem; many bed and breakfasts are owned by couples and serve as a second income. While one person works at another job, the other tends to the needs of the bed and breakfast.

The Professional Association of Innkeepers International (PAII), a professional association for the owners of bed and breakfasts and country inns, classifies the different kinds of bed and breakfasts. A *host home* is considered a very small business with only a few rooms for rent. Because of its small size, the owner of a host home may not be required by law to license the business or to have government inspections. Without advertising or signs, these homes are referred to guests primarily through reservation service organizations (RSO). A *bed and breakfast* and *bed and breakfast inn* are classified as having 4 to 20 rooms. They adhere to license, inspection, and zoning requirements and promote their businesses through brochures, print ads, and signs. A *country inn* is considered a bit larger, with 6 to 30 rooms, and it may serve one meal in addition to breakfast.

Requirements

High School

Because you'll essentially be maintaining a home as a bed and breakfast owner, you should take home economics courses. These courses can prepare you for the requirements of shopping and cooking for a group of people as well as budgeting household finances. But a bed and breakfast is also a business, so you need to further develop those budgeting skills in a business fundamentals class, accounting, and math. A shop class, or some other hands-on workshop, can be very valuable to you; take a class that will teach you about electrical wiring, woodworking, and other elements of home repair.

Postsecondary Training

As a bed and breakfast owner, you're in business for yourself, so there are no educational requirements for success. Also, no one specific degree program will better prepare you than any other. A degree in history or art may be as valuable as a degree in business management. Before taking over a bed and breakfast, though, you may consider enrolling in a hotel management or small business program at your local community college. Such programs can educate you in the practical aspects of running a bed and breakfast, from finances and loans to health and licensing regulations.

Opportunities for part-time jobs and internships with a bed and breakfast are few and far between. Bed and breakfast owners can usually use extra help during busy seasons, but can't always afford to hire a staff. But some do enough business that they can hire a housekeeper or a secretary, or they may have an extra room to provide for an apprentice willing to help with the business.

Certification or Licensing

Though bed and breakfast owners aren't generally certified or licensed as individuals, they do license their businesses, and seek accreditation for their inns from professional organizations such as PAII and the American Bed and Breakfast Association. With accreditation, the business can receive referrals from the associations and can be included in their directories. A house with only a room or two for rent may not be subject to any licensing requirements, but most bed and breakfasts are state regulated. A bed and breakfast owner must follow zoning regulations, maintain a small business license, pass health inspections, and carry sufficient liability insurance.

Other Requirements

Bed and breakfast ownership calls upon diverse skills—you must have a head for business, but you have to be comfortable working among people outside of an office. You must be creative in the way you maintain the house, paying attention to decor and gardening, but you should also have practical skills in plumbing and other household repair (or you should at least be capable of diagnosing any need for repair). A knowledge of the electrical wiring of your house and the phone lines is valuable. You'll also need an ability to cook well for groups both large and small.

"I'm easygoing," Mark says in regards to how he makes his business a success, "and I know how to set, and follow through on, personal and professional goals. I'm also a natural organizer, and pay attention to details." Mark also enjoys meeting new people, which is very important. You'll be expected to be a gracious host to all your guests. But you'll also have to maintain rules and regulations; guests of bed and breakfasts expect a quiet environment, and smoking and drinking is often prohibited.

If turning your home into a bed and breakfast, you should learn about city planning and zoning restrictions, as well as inspection programs. Computer skills will help you to better organize reservations, registration histories, and tax records. You should have some knowledge of marketing in order to promote your business by ad, brochure, and on the Internet.

Exploring

The PAII provides students with a free informational packet about innkeeping, and also puts together an "Aspiring Innkeepers Package" for those interested in the requirements of running a bed and breakfast. PAII publishes a newsletter and books on innkeeping, holds conferences, and maintains a very informative Web site. If there are inns in your town, interview the owners and spend a day or two with them as they perform their daily duties. The owner may even have part-time positions open for someone to assist with preparing breakfast or cleaning the rooms—employment of staff has increased in the last few years. Some bed and breakfast owners occasionally hire reliable "innsitters" to manage their inns when they're out of town.

Even a job as a motel housekeeper or desk clerk can give you experience with the responsibilities of innkeeping. Bed and breakfasts, hotels, and resorts across the country often advertise nationally for seasonal assistance. For years, high school and college students have made a little extra money working in exotic locales by dedicating their summers to full-time hotel or resort jobs. Wait staff, poolside assistants, kitchen staff, housekeepers, and spa assistants are needed in abundance during peak tourist seasons. In some cases, you can get a paid position, and in others you may be expected to work in exchange for room and board. Even if your summer job is at a large resort rather than a small bed and breakfast, you can still develop valuable people skills and learn a lot about the travel and tourism industry.

Employers

Innkeepers work for themselves. The charm of bed and breakfasts is that they are owned and operated by individuals, or individual families, who live on the premises. Though bed and breakfast "chains" may be a thing of the future, they are not expected to greatly affect the business of the traditional "mom and pop" operations.

Most bed and breakfasts exist in rural areas and small towns where there are no large hotels. Though the number of inns in cities is increasing, only 21 percent of the inns in the United States are located in urban areas. According to the PAII, the majority of inns (53 percent) are in small resort villages. Twenty-six percent of the inns are in rural areas.

An innkeeper's income is derived from room rental and fees for any "extras" such as additional meals and transportation. An inn's guests are often from outside of the local area, but an inn may also cater to many area residents. Most guests are screened by reservation service organizations or travel associations; this helps to protect both the guest and the owner. Bed and breakfasts must pass certain approval requirements, and guests must prove to be reliable, paying customers.

Starting Out

Probably all the bed and breakfast owners you speak to will have different stories about how they came to own their businesses. Some, like Mark, convert their own homes into inns; others buy fully established businesses, complete with client lists, marketing plans, and furnishings. Others inherit their bed and breakfasts from family members. And still others lease a house from another owner. Usually, bed and breakfast ownership requires large investment, both in time and money. Before starting your business, you must do a great deal of research. Make sure the local market can support an additional bed and breakfast and that your house and grounds will offer a unique and attractive alternative to the other lodging in the area. Research how much you can expect to make the first few years, and how much you can afford to lose. Mark suggests that you be sure to promote your business, but don't go overboard. "All advertising is not worth it," he says. "I have found that small ads in local publications, one listing in a nationally distributed magazine, a home or Web page, and word of mouth are more than enough."

Established bed and breakfasts for sale are advertised nationally, and by innkeeper associations. Prices range from under $100,000 to over $1,000,000. An established business is often completely restored and includes antique furniture and fixtures, as well as necessary equipment.

Advancement

Mark sees expansion in the future of the Dillinger House Bed and Breakfast. "I see buying another property in the neighborhood," he says, "and at that point operating as an inn/spa. This would enable me to hire a small staff and include some of the extras for my guests to make them feel even more pampered." With the free time that a staff would provide, Mark could dedicate more time to marketing and promotion.

In many cases, a married bed and breakfast owner may continue to work full-time outside of the home, while his or her spouse sees to the daily concerns of the inn. But once a business is well-established with a steady clientele, both spouses may be able to commit full-time to the bed and breakfast.

Earnings

Large, well-established bed and breakfasts can bring in thousands of dollars every year, but most owners of average sized inns must make do with much less. A survey by the PAII provides a variety of income figures. A beginning bed and breakfast has an annual net operating income of $25,000, while one 7 years or older has an average income of over $73,000. A small bed and breakfast with 4 rooms or fewer for rent has an annual net income of about $7,000; an inn of 5 to 8 rooms has an income of $35,000; 9 to 12 rooms, $80,000. An inn with 13 to 20 rooms has a net operating income of over $168,000.

Bed and breakfasts in the western part of the United States make more money than those in other parts of the country. An average net income of $68,000 per year is figured for inns in the West, followed by $58,000 for those in the Northeast, $38,000 in the Southeast, and $33,000 in the Midwest. Bed and breakfasts charge from $80 to $120 per day, depending on size of the room and whether it has a private bath, fireplace, and other amenities.

Work Environment

Imagine yourself living in a beautiful, restored historical house among antiques and vacationers from all around the world. And you don't have to leave to go to work. Though it sounds like an ideal environment, and it may not seem like you're at work, you will be performing many responsibilities to keep the house nice and pleasant. Your chores will mostly be domestic ones, keeping you close to the house with cooking, cleaning, gardening, and laundering. This makes for a very comfortable work environment over which you have a great deal of control. Your workplace will likely remain calm and quiet, with a short time of hustle and bustle in the morning as guests take their breakfast and prepare for their days. Though you'll be working in your own home, you must sacrifice much of your privacy to operate a bed and breakfast. You'll be expected to be available to your guests and to see to their comfort their entire stay with you. However, even the most successful bed and breakfast isn't always full to capacity, and many are only open on weekends—this may result in a few long work days, then a few days all to yourself. But to keep your business afloat, you'll want to welcome as many guests as you can handle.

Outlook

Some bed and breakfasts have been in business for decades, but it's only been in the last 20 years that inns have become popular vacation spots. PAII estimates the number of inns in the country to be between 15,000 and 20,000, up from a measly 5,000 in 1980. Tourists are seeking out inns as inexpensive and charming alternatives to the rising cost and sterile, cookie-cutter design of hotels and motels. People are even centering their vacation plans on bed and breakfasts, booking trips to historical towns for restful departures from cities. As long as bed and breakfasts can keep their rates lower than hotel chains, they are likely to flourish.

Recognizing the appeal of bed and breakfasts, some hotel chains are considering plans to capitalize on the trend with "inn-style" lodging. An inn-style hotel is even on its way to Disneyland! Smaller hotels composed of larger, suite-style rooms with more personalized service may threaten the business of some bed and breakfasts. But the charm and historic significance of an old house can't easily be reproduced, so bed and breakfasts are expected to maintain their niche in the tourism industry.

The Americans with Disabilities Act (ADA) will also have some effect on the future of bed and breakfasts. Inns with more than six rooms are required to comply with the ADA, making their rooms and grounds handicapped accessible. When purchasing a property for the purpose of a bed and breakfast, buyers must take into consideration the expense and impact of making such additions and changes. Though some businesses may have trouble complying, those that can will open up an area of tourism previously unavailable to people with disabilities.

For More Information

Contact PAII and request their free student packet. It contains information about innkeepers and their guests, lists of seminars and consultants, and the results of a study detailing average operating expenses and revenues.

Professional Association of Innkeepers International
PO Box 90710
Santa Barbara, CA 93190
Tel: 805-569-1853
Email: info@paii.org
Web: http://www.paii.org

For information on state associations and tips on opening your own B & B, contact:

American Bed and Breakfast Association
Email: info@abba.com
Web: http://www.abba.com/

Caterers

	School Subjects
Business Family and consumer science	
	Personal Skills
Artistic Helping/teaching	
	Work Environment
Primarily indoors Primarily multiple locations	
	Minimum Education Level
Some postsecondary training	
	Salary Range
$15,000 to $30,000 to $75,000	
	Certification or Licensing
Required by certain states	
	Outlook
Faster than the average	

Overview

Caterers plan, coordinate, and supervise food service at parties and at other social functions. Working with their clients, they purchase appropriate supplies, plan menus, supervise food preparation, direct serving of food and refreshments, and ensure the overall smooth functioning of the event. As entrepreneurs, they are also responsible for budgeting, bookkeeping, and other administrative tasks.

History

In Europe in the 16th century, cooking developed into an art form. Royalty and aristocrats sought out the finest chefs to cook for important events. By the late 1700s, restaurants and hotels opened, offering the cooking of talented chefs to a larger population. Hotels expanded into luxury establishments complete with banquet halls. When renting a hall for an event, people could take advantage of the cooking skills of the hotel chefs. Antonin Careme of France was one of the first chefs to gain worldwide fame; he created and perfected recipes and cooking techniques, wrote cookbooks, and served world leaders. Germain Charles Chevet opened many food shops in Paris, and catered events offering his special preparations of venison and seafood. The 1800s also saw improved methods of preserving foods through canning and refrigeration, and advances in stoves and ovens which assisted in quicker food preparation. By the 1930s, ranges and refrigerators were in common use, and World War II spurred further advances in food preservation in order to feed the soldiers. All these advances assisted chefs in the preparation and transportation of food, allowing them to cater events at some distance from their kitchens.

The Job

As a caterer, you'll be moving from kitchen, to serving tray, to your personal computer. A caterer is a chef, purchasing agent, personnel director, and accountant. Often you'll play the role of host, allowing clients to enjoy their own party. Your responsibilities vary depending on the size of the catering firm and the specific needs of individual clients. While preparing quality food is a concern no matter what the size of the party, larger events require far more planning and coordination. For example, you may organize and plan a formal event for a thousand people, including planning and preparing a 7-course meal, decorating the hall with flowers and wall hangings, employing 20 or more wait staff to serve food, and arranging the entertainment. You'll also set up the tables and chairs and provide the necessary linen, silverware, and dishes. You may organize 50 or so such events a month or only several a year. A smaller catering organization may concentrate on simpler events, such as preparing food for an informal buffet for 15 people. In addition to individual clients, you may also choose to serve industrial clients. You may supervise a company cafeteria or plan food service for an airline or cruise ship.

Cary Farley, owner of All the Trimmings Catering in the Twin Cities of Minnesota, prefers to keep her business and staff small. She prefers to cater dinner parties for groups of 24 or less, rather than corporate parties. "When you get into doing very large groups," she says, "you can't afford to make all your own food." Cary offers her clients the Southern-style cooking she grew up with; some of her specialties, such as Sally Lunn bread (a light, hot-roll bread baked in an angel food cake pan), are even derived from family recipes. "Mini crab cakes with tarragon mayonnaise," Cary lists. "Grits Timbal with herbs and cheddar cheese. Chocolate truffle cake." Although as a caterer, you'll be preparing a variety of dishes, you may choose your own specialty, such as Cajun or Italian cuisine. You may also have a special serving style, such as serving food in Renaissance period dress, that sets you apart from other caterers. Developing a reputation by specializing in a certain area is an especially effective marketing technique.

You'll be preparing your specialties either in a commercial kitchen which meets your state's standards and requirements, or on location. When handling a large banquet in a hotel or other location, for example, you will usually prepare the food on-premises, using kitchen and storage facilities as needed. You might also work in a client's kitchen for an event in a private home. In both cases, you must visit the site of the function well before the actual event to determine how and where the food will be prepared.

Working with the client is obviously a very important aspect of the caterer's job. "My job is to showcase the host and hostess," Cary says, "so they can enjoy their own party, and their guests will remember them for it." Clients always want their affairs to be extra special, and the caterer's ability to present such items as a uniquely shaped wedding cake or to provide beautiful decorations will enhance the atmosphere and contribute to customer satisfaction. You'll work with your client to establish a budget, develop a menu, and determine the desired atmosphere. "I help the client come up with a menu, centerpieces, music, linen, the whole thing," Cary says. When catering an event, you'll work with suppliers, food servers, and the client to ensure an event comes off as planned. You must stay in frequent contact with all parties involved in the affair, making sure, for example, that the food is delivered on time, the flowers are fresh, and the entertainment shows up and performs as promised.

Throughout the party or dinner, you'll serve, fill glasses, and make sure the hot food stays hot and cold food stays cold. You'll also direct any staff you have assisting you. After the party, you'll clean up and pack your things. Once you've returned to your kitchen and home-based quarters, you'll then put away linens and serving pieces.

Good management skills are extremely important. You must know how much food and other supplies to order, what equipment will be needed, how many staff to hire, and be able to coordinate the various activities to ensure a smooth-running event. Purchasing proper supplies entails knowledge of a variety of food products, their suppliers, and the contacts needed to get the right product at the best possible price. You may also have to research recipes and customs when planning a special event. Cary recalls planning a Latvian wedding. "Online, I found two Latvian cooks right in the Twin Cities," she says. These cooks assisted in translating some recipes for her. "I use the computer a great deal," she adds. "With the Internet, I can look at the menus of restaurants all across the country." She also had some particular challenges when catering a party for the rock band, the B-52s. The band was in the city doing some concerts, and Cary had to come up with some vegetarian dishes.

Because you're running the business yourself, you'll be overseeing the budgeting and bookkeeping of the operation. You must make sure that the business continues to make a profit while keeping its prices competitive. You must know how to figure costs and other budgetary considerations, plan inventories, buy food, and ensure compliance with health regulations. You'll also be hiring additional staff to serve at special events.

Requirements

High School

In home economics courses, you'll learn the basics of cooking and nutrition, as well as household budgeting. You may also receive some instruction in table design and floral arrangement. Assist at school banquets and parties to get an idea of the demands of cooking for large groups of people. English courses can help you develop the communications skills you'll need for planning events with clients and promoting your services. Math and accounting courses will prepare you for the bookkeeping and administrative demands of the job.

Postsecondary Training

You don't have to go to college in order to start your own catering business, but many caterers have been to culinary schools, or have taken courses in small business management. Colleges across the country offer programs in catering management, hotel management, tourism and convention, and hospitality management. The National Association of Catering Executives (NACE) accredits schools with catering related programs. Courses include: economics, commercial food production, hospitality information systems, marketing, nutrition, and facilities planning. These programs may offer scholarships, as well as internship opportunities which offer hands-on training with professional caterers.

Certification or Licensing

Most states require caterers to be licensed, and inspectors may make periodic visits to catering operations to ensure that local health and safety regulations are being maintained in food preparation, handling, and storage. As a measure of professional status, many caterers become certified through the National Association of Catering Executives (NACE). To qualify for this certification, caterers must meet certain educational and professional requirements as well as pass a written examination. Further information on the certification process, as well as general career information, is available from NACE at the address given at the end of this article.

Other Requirements

Although there are no specific educational or professional requirements for this field, a professional caterer should be well-versed in proper food preparation techniques and be able to manage a food service operation. Many people develop these skills through on-the-job training, beginning as a caterer's helper or a restaurant worker.

Exploring

Contact local caterers about temporary work. Many caterers hire reliable people for busy weekends and holidays to assist with food preparation and serving. "I have several teenagers who work for me," Cary says. "Most caterers would love to have extra help." Part-time catering work usually pays better than baby-sitting and other jobs available to high school students on the weekends. You can also gain relevant experience with a part-time job in a restaurant as a waitperson or as an assistant banquet manager at a hotel.

Employers

You'll be catering for the parties and events of individuals, such as weddings, bar and bat mitzvahs, holiday parties, and anniversary celebrations. You'll also be working for corporations, catering office parties and conventions. Charity organizations may also hire you for dinners and fundraising events.

Though many large hotels have their own restaurant staff for large parties, they occasionally hire additional caterers to consult or assist on projects.

Starting Out

Cary had worked in health care management for 16 years before starting her catering business. When she received a severance package from the corporation, she knew she wanted to start a business. "I thought I wanted to own a bed and breakfast," she said. "But then I realized that I hate housework." The "breakfast" aspect of the b and b appealed to her, however, as she enjoyed cooking for people. She began working as a personal chef, then started catering parties. Her background in business has served her well; with a lot of experience in project management, she can handle the demands of catering an event.

Some caterers enter the profession as a matter of chance after helping a friend or relative prepare a large banquet or volunteering to coordinate a group function. Most caterers, however, begin their careers after graduating from college with a degree in a program such as home economics, or finishing a culinary training program at a vocational school or community college. An individual will most likely start a catering business only with extensive experience and sufficient finances to purchase equipment and meet other start-up costs. "I haunt second-hand shops and estate sales for pots and pans, serving pieces, and silver," Cary says.

Advancement

Your success as a caterer will depend on the quality of work and a good reputation. Well-known caterers can expand their businesses, often growing from a small business to a larger operation. This may mean hiring assistants and buying more equipment in order to be able to serve a larger variety of clientele. Caterers who initially worked out of their own home kitchens may get an office or relocate to another area in order to take advantage of better catering opportunities. Sometimes successful caterers use their skills and reputations to secure full-time positions in large hotels or restaurants as banquet coordinators and planners. Independent caterers may also secure contracts with industrial clients, such as airlines, hospitals, schools, and companies, to staff their cafeterias or supply food and beverages. They may also be employed by such companies to manage their food operations.

Earnings

Earnings vary widely depending on the size and location of the catering operation and the skill and motivation of the individual entrepreneur. Also, some caterers only work part-time, supplementing their income with restaurant cheffing, and related work. Many caterers charge according to the number of guests attending a function (generally $10 to $20 per person). Bill Hansen of The Leading Caterers of America (LCA) estimates that caterers take home 20 to 40 percent of the sales volume. Sales volume is the total amount of money a caterer takes in from parties and dinners. To determine income, you must subtract business expenses such as groceries and staff payment. A survey conducted by the National Caterers Association found there were two general ranges of sales volume: $100,000 to $400,000, and $1,000,000 to $2,000,000.

Full-time caterers can earn between $15,000 and $60,000 per year, depending on skill, reputation, and experience. An extremely successful caterer can easily earn more than $75,000 annually. A part-time caterer may earn $7,000 to $15,000 per year, subject to the same variables as the full-time caterer. Because most caterers are self-employed, vacations and other benefits are usually not part of the wage structure.

Work Environment

A caterer often works long hours planning and preparing for an event, and the day of the event might easily be a 14-hour workday from setup to cleanup. Caterers often spend long hours on their feet, and although the work can be physically and mentally demanding, caterers usually enjoy a great deal of work flexibility. As entrepreneurs, they can usually take time off when necessary. Caterers often work more than 60 hours a week during busy seasons, with most of the work on weekends and evenings, when events tend to be scheduled.

Caterers must be able to plan ahead, work gracefully under pressure, and have the ability to adapt to last minute mishaps. Attention to detail is critical, as is the ability to work long hours under demanding situations.

Caterers must be able to direct a large staff of kitchen workers and waitpersons and be able to interact well with clients, guests, and employees.

Outlook

Because of the strong food service industry in the United States, employment opportunities in catering should continue to grow. Opportunities will be good for firms that handle weddings, bar and bat mitzvahs, business functions, and other events. Large wedding anniversary celebrations have become more common.

Competition is keen as many hotels and restaurants branch out to offer catering services. Like all service industries, catering is sensitive to the economy, and a downturn in the economy may limit catering opportunities. Despite the competition and fluctuating economic conditions, highly skilled and motivated caterers should be in demand throughout the country, especially in and around large metropolitan areas.

For More Information

This trade association offers information on certification and other career information.

National Association of Catering Executives
60 Revere Drive, Suite 500
Northbrook, IL 60062
Tel: 847-480-9080
Web: http://www.nacefoundation.org

For extensive information about the industry, and information about publications and training, visit the LCA Web site, or contact:

Leading Caterers of America (LCA)
2167 South Bayshore Drive
Miami, FL 33133
Tel: 800-743-6660
Web: http://www.leadingcaterers.com

Child Care Service Owners

	School Subjects
Business **Family and consumer science**	
	Personal Skills
Helping/teaching **Leadership/management**	
	Work Environment
Primarily indoors Primarily one location	
	Minimum Education Level
Some postsecondary training	
	Salary Range
$20,000 to $30,000 to $50,000+	
	Certification or Licensing
Required by certain states	
	Outlook
Faster than the average	

Overview

A child care service provides care for infants, toddlers, and pre-school aged children. While the parents and guardians are at work, child care providers watch the children and help them develop skills through games and activities. The child care service may be part of the owner's home, or may be a separate center composed of classrooms, play areas, and areas for infant care. The service owner must hire, train, and schedule child care workers, or teachers, to assist with large numbers of children. The owner must also manage the center's finances, assure that the center meets legal requirements and accreditation standards, and meet with prospective clients. Child care centers are in demand all across the country, as the majority of parents of young children have jobs outside the home. There are over 2 million child care providers, workers, and pre-kindergarten teachers working in the United States. There are over 100,000 early child care centers in the country.

History

You probably think daytime child care is a fairly modern idea. It's true that only 17 percent of the mothers of one-year-olds were part of the labor force in 1965. That number seems small when you look at statistics from the U.S. Department of Labor—today, 6 of every 10 mothers of children under age 6 are working outside the home. But child care centers were needed as far back as the 18th century. In England, factories opened nurseries to care for the workers' children, a trend which carried over to the United States in the 19th century. Of course, working conditions in factories were often terrible before the 1900s, and the children were put to work at very young ages. So the child care service as we know it today didn't really begin to evolve until World War II, when women joined the work force while the men were off fighting. Though many of these women quit their jobs when the men returned from the war, roles for women began to change. The last half of the 20th century saw more opportunities for women in the workplace and, for many families, two incomes became necessary to meet the rising costs of living. Today, in 61 percent of the married couples in the United States, both the husband and the wife work outside the home. This has put dependable, safe, child care services in high demand.

The Job

You've probably had some experience with baby-sitting a few kids at a time. Now imagine yourself responsible for several children of various ages, every single work day. As the owner of a child care service, you take on the responsibility of providing quality care to young children. But the parents don't just expect you to keep an eye on the kids while they're at work—they also expect you to help the children learn basic skills and to prepare them for their first years of school. You'll come up with activities that build on children's abilities and curiosity. Attention to the individual needs of each child is important, so that you can adapt these activities to specific needs. For example, you should plan activities based on the understanding that a three-year-old child has different motor skills and reasoning abilities than a child of five years of age. Because you'll be caring for babies, toddlers, and kids of pre-kindergarten age, you'll be offering many different kinds of instruction. Some kids will just be learning how to tie their shoes and button their coats, while others will have begun to develop reading and computer skills. And, of course, the infants in your care will require less teaching and more individual attention—you'll assure that the babies are fed, diapered, and held when awake. If you own a large facility, you'll hire aides, teachers, and assistant directors to help you.

Nancy Moretti owns a child care center in Smithfield, Rhode Island, called Just For Kids. The center is licensed to care for 54 children, and is composed of 5 classrooms—each room for a different age group. She has a staff of 18 who work with kids from 6 weeks to 5 years old. "Everyone here loves children," Nancy says. "We're an extended family; we all look out for each other." Nancy's day starts with a walk through the classrooms to make sure everything is in order, and to make sure all the staff members and children are there. Much of Nancy's work consists of attending to staff concerns, such as payment and scheduling. When hiring teachers for her center, she looks for people with some background in child development, such as a college degree or some years of practical experience.

When working with children, you'll rely on a background in child development to create a flexible schedule allowing time for music, art, playtime, academics, rest, and other activities. You and your staff will work with the youngest children to teach them the days of the week and to recognize colors, seasons, and animal names and characteristics; you'll help older children with number and letter recognition and simple writing skills. Self-confidence and the development of communications skills are encouraged in day care centers. For example, you may give children simple art projects, such as finger painting and have children show and explain their finished projects to the rest of the class. Show and tell gives students opportunities to speak and listen to others. You'll also help children with such tasks as picking up their toys and washing their hands before snack time.

But you'll have many other responsibilities aside from lessons and instruction. If you've worked with children at all, you know they need a lot of assistance in a variety of ways. A major portion of a child care worker's day is spent helping children adjust to being away from home and encouraging them to play together. You'll gently reassure children who become frightened or homesick. You'll help kids with their coats and boots in the winter time, and also deal with the sniffles, colds, and generally cranky behavior that can occur in young children. You'll supervise snack time, teaching children how to eat properly and clean up after themselves.

You'll also work with the parents of each child. It is not unusual for parents to come to preschool and observe a child or go on a field trip with the class, and child care workers often take these opportunities to discuss the progress of each child as well as any specific problems or concerns. Scheduled meetings are available for parents who cannot visit the school during the day. Nancy makes it a point to be frequently available for the parents when they're dropping off, and picking up, the children. "Parents need to know that I'm here," she says. "For the owner to be involved is important to the parents."

Requirements

High School

You should take courses in early childhood development, when available. Many home economics courses include units in parenting and child care. English courses will help you to develop communication skills important in dealing with children, their parents, and a child care staff. In teaching children, you should be able to draw from a wide base of education and interests, so take courses in art, music, science, and physical education. Math and accounting courses will prepare you for the bookkeeping and management requirements of running your own business.

Postsecondary Training

A college degree isn't required for you to open a daycare center, but can serve you in a variety of ways. A child development program will give you the background needed for classroom instruction, as well as for understanding the basics of child care and psychology. A college degree will also demonstrate to your clients that you have the background necessary for good child care. A college degree program should include coursework in a variety of liberal arts subjects, including English, history, and science, as well as nutrition, child development, psychology of the young child, and sociology.

Certification or Licensing

Requirements for child care workers vary from state to state. Some states require that you complete a certain number of continuing education hours every year; these hours may include college courses or research into the subject of child care. CPR training is also often required. National certification isn't required of child care service owners and workers, but some organizations do offer it. The Council for Early Childhood Professional Recognition offers the Child Development Associate (CDA) National Credentialing Program. To become a CDA, you must meet competency standards and have experience in child care. There are over 100,000 CDAs across the country. The National Child Care Association offers the Certified Childcare Professional (CCP) Credential. To receive this credential, you must have extensive child care experience, along with special training.

Other Requirements

Obviously, a love for children and a concern for their care and safety are most important. Child care comes naturally to most of those who run child care services. "I can't see myself doing anything but this," Nancy says. You should be very patient, and capable of teaching children in many different stages of development. Because young children look up to adults and learn through example, it is important that a child care worker be a good role model—you should treat the children with respect and kindness, while also maintaining order and control. You must also be good at communicating with the parents, capable of addressing their concerns, and keeping them informed as to their children's progress.

Exploring

You can gain experience in this field by volunteering at a child care center or other preschool facility. Some high schools provide internships with local preschools for students interested in working as a teacher's aide. Your guidance counselor can provide information on these opportunities. Summer day camps or Bible schools with preschool classes also hire high school students as counselors or counselors-in-training. Take tours of child care centers of various sizes, and talk to the owners about how they started their businesses.

Employers

No matter where you set up shop, you'll be able to find clients. If buying an established day care facility, most of your clients will come along with it. If starting your own center, you'll rely on word-of-mouth, and you'll offer your services to people you know. Though franchise opportunities failed in the industry 20 years ago, franchising is again becoming a viable option. Child care franchising operations are among the fastest growing organizations in the industry. Primrose Schools and Kids 'R Kids International, are a few of the child care companies offering franchises.

In some cases, people work from their homes, watching only their own children and some of the children from their neighborhoods; this is usually referred to as "family child care." Quality child care is a concern of most parents, regardless of economic standing. Single working mothers are often the hardest hit with child care expenses, and recent federal mandates requiring states to find work for welfare recipients means even more children needing daytime care outside the home. Government programs and subsidies help to provide child care services for lower-income families.

Starting Out

At your first opportunity, you should take part-time work at a child care center to gain first-hand experience. Contact child care centers, nursery schools, Head Start programs, and other preschool facilities to learn about job opportunities. Often there are many jobs for child care workers listed in the classified sections of newspapers. The Child Care Bureau estimates that one-third of all child care teachers leave their centers each year. "You need to make sure child care is something you want to do," Nancy says, "before starting your own center." Some owners of child care centers are not actively involved with the day-to-day running of the business; parents, however, prefer to leave their children at a center where the owner takes an active interest in each child's well-being. Nancy purchased a day care center that had been in operation for nearly 10 years, and she had worked as a teacher and director at that center for 8 of them. Knowing all the parents already helped her ease into ownership without losing a single client. When buying an established daycare center, Nancy recommends that you spend a few months getting to know the parents first.

Advancement

As your center becomes better known in the community, and as you gain a reputation for providing quality child care, you may be able to expand your business. With enough income, you can hire staff members to help with the child care, instruction, and the administrative requirements. Nancy is currently in the process of expanding Just For Kids in a variety of ways. She'll be putting an addition onto the building to allow for a number of new services: a full-day kindergarten, a before- and after-school program, and a summer day camp. Nancy also recently sent surveys out to the parents to determine whether Saturday child care is needed.

A 1998 status report by the Child Care Information Exchange found that 30 percent of the child care organizations surveyed planned to offer elementary school services by the end of that year. Parents want to stay as active in their children's grade school education as they are in their pre-school care. Therefore, child centers are beginning to offer instruction for children into the 8th grade and further.

Earnings

It is difficult to determine exact salaries for child care service owners since revenue for child care centers varies according to the number of children cared for, whether the center is owned or rented, number of staff, and other factors. A large percentage, approximately 70 percent, of a child care center's expenses go to paying the staff. The Child Care Information Exchange published the results of various studies on the cost of center-based child care: the annual budget for a typical child care center serving 65 children is $330,000, which includes labor, occupancy, supplies, and food. To care for a one-year-old child, a center will charge weekly rates of $90 to $200. A center in a city with a higher cost of living and more staffing and licensing requirements will charge more than a center in a smaller town. Centers generally charge less for older children. A center will charge per hour for school age children—$2.50 to $4.50.

According to the Child Care Bureau, child care workers with high school diplomas have average annual earnings of $10,151. Workers with some college credits earn around $11,617 a year, and those holding college degrees earn an average of $14,506 a year.

Work Environment

You'll be spending a lot of time on your feet directing children and checking on classrooms. Most child care centers have play areas both inside and outside. In the spring and summer months, you may spend some time outside with the kids, leading them in playground exercises. The colder winter months will keep you and the kids confined mostly to the indoors. Though child care workers can control the noise somewhat, the work conditions are rarely quiet. Depending on the size of your center, your work will be divided between child care and administrative responsibilities; you will have some time in your office attending to business matters and making phone calls. Nancy's center is open Monday through Friday, 6:30 AM to 6:00 PM, but she also works weekends. "It's fun most of the time," she says, despite 70 to 80 hour work weeks.

Outlook

Employment opportunities for preschool teachers are expected to increase through the year 2006. More women than ever are part of the workforce; of those who have children, many take only an abbreviated maternity leave. The Children's Defense League states that over 13 million children in the United States are in day care every work day, and most of these children were enrolled in child care by the time they were 3 months old. Corporations have tried to open their own day care centers for the children of employees, but haven't had much success. These corporations will contract with outside day care centers to meet these child care needs.

Independently owned, "mom and pop" child care centers will remain very competitive in the market place, despite the presence of large chains. Though chains expect more rapid growth in the near future, they won't likely grow at the rate they did in the 1980s.

Well over 90 percent of people employed in child care occupations are female. Child care organizations are making efforts to encourage more men to become involved in the profession. Staffing problems in general plague the child care industry, as centers struggle to find reliable, long-term employees. Other concerns of child care organizations include providing better child care for low-income families; requiring more bilingual education; and making child care more inclusive for children with disabilities.

For More Information

For information about certification, contact:

Council for Early Childhood Professional Recognition
2460 16th Street, NW
Washington, DC 20009
Tel: 202-265-9090
Web: http://www.cdacouncil.org

For information about certification and to learn about the issues affecting child care, visit the NCCA Web page, or contact:

National Child Care Association
1016 Rosser Street
Conyers, GA 30012
Tel: 800-543-7161
Web: http://www.nccanet.org

For information about student memberships and training opportunities, contact:

National Association of Child Care Professionals
304-A Roanoke Street
Christiansburg, VA 24073
Tel: 800-537-1118
Web: http://www.naccp.org

Visit the NAEYC Web site to read relevant articles concerning issues of child care, and to learn about membership and accreditation.

National Association for the Education of Young Children
1509 16th Street, NW
Washington, DC 20036
Tel: 800-424-2460
Web: http://www.naeyc.org

Chimney Sweeps

	School Subjects
Business Chemistry Technical/Shop	

	Personal Skills
Mechanical/manipulative Technical/scientific	

	Work Environment
Primarily multiple locations Indoors and outdoors	

	Minimum Education Level
Apprenticeship	

	Salary Range
$11,000 to $23,000 to $45,000+	

	Certification or Licensing
Recommended	

	Outlook
About as fast as the average	

Overview

Chimney sweeps, also known as *sweeps* and *chimney technicians,* inspect—or evaluate, as it is known in the industry—chimneys, fireplaces, stoves, and vents according to safety codes. They clean, or sweep, the chimneys and make repairs, which may involve masonry work and relining. They also educate homeowners and building maintenance crews in how to properly care for their stoves and fireplaces, as well as train apprentice chimney sweeps. In the United States and Canada, there are between 6,000 and 6,500 chimney sweeps. They work in every region of the country.

History

The traditional image of the soot-faced chimney sweep in top hat and tails, carrying a long brush, is still very much a part of the chimney sweep industry. Many chimney sweep businesses and organizations use the image in advertising and logos, including the National Chimney Sweep Guild

(NCSG). The sweep of popular imagination originated in the city of pre-industrial London, with its tight rows of brick houses. Before the introduction of central heating, chimney sweeps thrived. The sweep took on an almost mythical quality, leaping from roof to roof, chimney pot to chimney pot. Unfortunately, the industry didn't have the safety codes, equipment, and technology of today, which resulted in health hazards. Cancer and other illnesses particularly affected the small boys and girls who, long before child labor laws, were cruelly sent into the chimneys to do the work a brush couldn't. Today's chimney sweep, however, working under the strict codes of the National Fire Protection Association, is more closely associated with health—their evaluations and repairs save lives and homes from destruction by fire.

Though chimney sweeping has a long tradition, only in the last 30 years has it developed as a modern career choice. The energy crisis of the early 1970s resulted in many homeowners converting from central heat to fireplaces and stoves. The popularity of wood burning stoves has waned somewhat since then because of fears of fire and carbon monoxide poisoning, but the chimney sweep industry is hard at work to educate the public about advances in the technology and equipment that keeps fireplaces and chimneys perfectly safe.

The Job

The Chimney Safety Institute of America (CSIA) estimates that in 1992, a particularly devastating year for house fires, 39,200 residential fires originated in chimneys, fireplaces, and solid fuel appliances. These fires resulted in 290 injuries, 90 deaths, and $206 million in property damage. It's no wonder then, that many chimney sweeps have worked as firefighters. With an understanding of the damage a chimney fire can do to a home, sweeps not only keep chimneys safer, they also serve as advocates for fire prevention.

The National Fire Protection Association recommends that homeowners have their chimneys, fireplaces, and vents evaluated at least once a year. Just as a dentist will send out annual reminder cards, so does John Pilger, the owner and operator of Chief Chimney Services, Inc. John Pilger sweeps, restores, relines, and waterproofs the chimneys of Brentwood, New York, and surrounding areas. "The work used to be seasonal," John says, "but more people are recognizing the need for chimney upkeep, so I work year-round."

Sweeps clean flues and remove creosote. Creosote is a residue that develops from wood and smoke and glazes the bricks of the insides of chimneys; sometimes chemicals are required to break down creosote. Sweeps also install stoves and perform a number of different repairs. People contact chimney sweeps with specific problems, such as too much smoking from the fireplace, or rain and snow getting in through the chimney. A sweep will attach a "cap" at the chimney top to prevent moisture, animals, and debris from entering the chimney. Crown repair also may be needed to keep the rain out.

Carbon monoxide poisoning is another concern of homeowners— sweeps reline deteriorating chimneys to keep carbon monoxide from seeping through into the home. With their masonry skills, chimney sweeps perform much brick repair and replacement. But sweeps don't just keep the home fires burning safely; they also attend to the chimneys and stoves of commercial businesses and industrial buildings. Some sweeps even specialize in the maintenance of the large smokestacks of electric and gas companies, which often involves traveling to multiple cities all across the country.

John makes four to seven stops in a work day. He usually makes it to his first customer's house between 8:30 and 9:00 AM. Once there, he'll spend from one to one-and-a-half hours sweeping the customer's oil or gas chimney, examining and sweeping the fireplace, and checking brickwork inside and out. He also does a video scan of the chimney, using equipment composed of a camera at the end of a pole. Despite such state of the art equipment, John says, "We haven't even touched the future of chimney technology."

The tools of the trade have advanced a great deal since the days of the 18th century when white geese were sent through chimneys; sweeps would determine how much creosote was inside the chimney from how darkly the geese's feathers were soiled. These days, in addition to the brushes, poles, and ladders that have long been necessary for cleaning, sweeps rely on a number of power tools. "From a demolition jackhammer to a cordless drill," John says. John owns special vacuums, hand grinders, and circular saws with diamond-tipped blades. "The blades are expensive and may only last three to four months," John says. But most of the tools, if treated well, can last a long time. John once had two trucks and four employees, but he decided he preferred to do the work himself. "It drove me crazy to get complaints," he says. So John and his wife, Diane, also a certified chimney sweep, now operate the business entirely themselves.

Some chimney sweeps sell a number of products. They sell wood and gas stoves, cook stoves, and gas barbecues. They sell fireplace inserts, fireplace glass doors, and gas logs. As with any small business, chimney sweeping involves a fair amount of office work. Detailed billing and client records must be kept, and customer phone calls must be answered and returned. Sweeps must also market their services. Many sweeps work to educate their communities on fire safety by distributing brochures and speaking at public events. John is a past president of the New York State Chimney Sweeps Guild, and he sits on the boards of directors of the NCSG and the CSIA.

Requirements

High School

To understand the damage done to chimneys by smoke, fire, and creosote, take science courses—particularly chemistry classes. In chemistry class, you'll learn more about the chemical reactions from fireplaces, such as carbon monoxide, that can cause illness and death if not contained. You may also be working with some chemicals to break down creosote glaze. With a clear understanding of the chemistry involved, you can easily explain problems to customers and stress the importance of chimney sweeping and repair.

In business courses, you can learn about marketing, budgeting, tax requirements, insurance, and other details of small business management. A computer course will give you some experience with databases, spread sheets, and other programs that assist in record-keeping and billing.

Postsecondary Training

The Chimney Safety Institute of America, the educational branch of the NCSG, actively trains sweeps and venting specialists and provides information to the general public about chimney safety. A training school, to be located near the NCSG headquarters in Indianapolis, is currently under development. CSIA offers a number of workshops and seminars all across the country, which introduce new sweeps to the business and provide continuing education to established sweeps. Training in such subjects as safety codes, environmental protection requirements, chimney construction, and technique helps sweeps prepare for the difficult CSIA certification exam.

No college degree is required, but community college courses in small business management, or tech school training in brickwork can help you prepare for ownership of your own chimney sweep service. Some experienced sweeps may even take you on as an apprentice; though the opportunity may not pay anything, it will provide you with valuable experience and education, and help you in your pursuit of certification. Many chimney sweeps have worked as firefighters or in other aspects of fire control and prevention. You may consider applying to the state fire academy for their extensive training. With experience in fire fighting, you'll learn to recognize fire hazards, which is important knowledge for sweeps.

Certification or Licensing

Certification isn't required to work as a chimney sweep, but is highly recommended by professionals in the industry. In its education of the public regarding chimney safety, the CSIA strongly advises homeowners to use only the services of certified sweeps. An unskilled sweep may be unable to recognize the potential for fire and health hazards in a deteriorating chimney and may even do more damage in the sweeping and repairing process. The CSIA certification exam is a difficult, 100-question test and requires complete knowledge of safety codes.

With certification, you can offer your clients additional security, and you can also receive referrals from the NCSG. Certification is valid for three years, after which you can re-test or attend CSIA-approved continuing education programs. Currently, the state of Vermont requires that only certified sweeps work with commercial and apartment buildings. Five other states are planning to follow suit.

Liability insurance is also important for chimney sweeps. Some sweeps have been named in lawsuits following fires in homes they serviced. Even if a sweep alerts a homeowner to potential hazards and the homeowner chooses not to have the work done, the sweep may be held liable if he or she didn't document the warning.

Other Requirements

You should have good technical and mechanical skills as you'll be working with power tools and construction. Patience is important because replacing linings and tiles and removing hard, glazed creosote can be time-consuming and tedious. Communication skills are valuable as you'll need to clearly explain to your clients the repairs needed and how to maintain a safe hearth. "Good customer service is very important," John emphasizes. His outgoing personality and background in customer relations helps him to attract clients and to keep them. He also once worked as a fire chief, and this background in dealing with fire hazards and educating the public about fire safety has served him well.

Exploring

Contact the NCSG for the names of chimney sweeps in your area, and look in the yellow pages of your phone book. A local sweep may allow you to follow him or her around for a day or two. Because of a shortage of chimney sweeps in the country, many sweeps and sweep organizations are anxious to recruit young people into the business. Speak to an NCSG representative about apprenticeship opportunities, or find one on your own by speaking to the sweeps in your town. The CSIA can also direct you to nearby educational seminars and conferences. By attending a conference, you'll get inside information about the business, and also get to talk with experienced chimney sweeps. There are a few publications devoted to chimney sweeping: *Sweeping,* the technical publication of the NCSG, *SNEWS—The Chimney Sweep News,* and *Chimney Topics.*

Employers

According to the NCSG, there are 6,000 to 6,500 chimney sweeps working in the United States and Canada. Ninety-five percent of the chimney sweep services are made up of three or fewer people. Many of them are literally "mom and pop" businesses, with pop tending to the chimney sweeping, and mom managing the office and telephone. Sweeps are in business in every region of the country, but fare the best in larger cities, or areas with an affluent suburban or rural area. Some sweeps work only within a specific area, while others may travel to smaller towns and into the country where no other services may be available.

Starting Out

Having developed experience as a fire chief, John bought a few chimney service companies and went into business. "The business can be as big or as small as you want it to be," John says. Though he has had a few employees in the past, he prefers to keep all the work for himself and his wife, therefore maintaining a smaller, more manageable business.

The equipment you need, which includes a truck, power tools, and other special equipment as well as protective gear, will be costly at first. You may have to work for a few years with another business, saving up money and building a list of reliable, paying customers. Once you've gained experience with chimney sweeping and have taken certification courses, you may be able to hire on with a large sweep service or to go into business with another sweep. Large businesses that sell and install wood and gas stoves will probably hire assistants, as will masonry businesses. Some of these businesses will advertise jobs in the classifieds, but your best bet would be to contact them directly. The CSIA seminars and conferences can help you get to know other chimney sweeps, both new and established, who could prove to be valuable contacts.

Advancement

Once you've established your own chimney sweep service, you can advance by making more connections in the community and expanding your client base. If the amount of work warrants it, you may choose to hire assistants and office staff. With a successful business, you can also afford the best equipment and the newest tools. You should attend the seminars and conferences offered by the CSIA to learn about the advances in technology for the industry. You can also advance your business by expanding the services offered. Some sweeps move into other areas of home repair, or they offer chimney and fireplace products for sale.

Earnings

The NCSG says salaries for chimney sweeps are too variable to estimate. Charges for services are also difficult to gauge. Sweeps working in larger cities and affluent neighborhoods can make much more for their services than those working in less populated areas. Sweeps charge anywhere from $50 to $100 for an annual cleaning, and $50 to $100 for a chimney cap. In areas where many people use stoves and fireplaces to heat their homes, such as in the New England states or the Northwest, a sweep may have four or more cleanings scheduled for every workday. In other parts of the country, the work may be seasonal, the bulk of servicing done in the months following the heating season. In addition to service fees, some sweeps also make money from the sales of stoves and fireplace products.

Work Environment

You'll be working both indoors and out. Some desk work is required to manage scheduling and finances, but most of your time will be spent climbing and bending, working in and around the homes of your customers. You'll be climbing ladders to the roofs of the homes to sweep and evaluate, and you'll spend some time down at the hearth within the home. The work can be noisy, due to the power tools and vacuums you'll be using, and it can be dirty and messy as well. You'll need to wear protective gear to prevent health problems. You will also be carrying the equipment from your truck to the home.

Though some established sweeps can afford to set their own schedules, working whatever hours they choose, others must be flexible to best accommodate their customers. A sweep may work an average 40-hour workweek, with a 24-hour phone number for emergency situations. You'll probably be doing much of the work by yourself, but some sweeps work as members of small teams. You'll also be working with your customers to establish good, continuing client relationships.

Outlook

The United States is likely to follow the advances made by European countries in environmental testing and protection. The NCSG closely follows these advanced practices and actively promotes new standards to the National Fire Protection Association and other agencies. In Germany, for example, homeowners are required by law to keep their chimneys within code. It may not come to that here, with organizations such as CSIA and the Hearth Education Foundation working hard to increase awareness of the many dangers of faulty chimneys.

With more rigid emissions testing expected in the United States, more home and business owners will call upon sweeps for chimney evaluations. Some states are beginning to require that chimney sweeps be CSIA-certified before working on commercial and apartment buildings. This will result in more sweeps becoming certified and better regulation of the industry. Along with new emissions standards, the industry will also benefit from technology in such areas as gas usage, more efficient appliances, and better water repellants.

For More Information

To learn about the industry and educational conferences and seminars in your area, contact the NCSG and its educational branch, the Chimney Safety Institute of America (http://www.csia.org).

National Chimney Sweep Guild
8752 Robbins Road
Indianapolis, IN 46268
Tel: 317-871-0030
Web: http://www.ncsg.org

Cleaning Service Owners

Overview

Cleaning service owners go into homes, offices, and apartment buildings to clean carpets, upholstery, and drapes. With special training, they also clean air ducts and restore homes and buildings damaged by fire, flood, and other disasters. There are successful cleaning services all across the country, but those businesses devoted to disaster restoration are generally located in areas with cold seasons and inclement weather.

History

Before the development of special looms and fibers, carpets and rugs were only for the well-to-do. A rug cleaner had to be very knowledgeable about the weaving and knotting of rugs, and about coloring and dying processes in order to properly clean and repair rugs. With the invention of "tufting" and synthetic fibers in Georgia in the 1930s, carpet production became more efficient, carpets became cheaper, and sales increased. And carpet cleaning became a service needed in homes and office buildings. Window washing companies were already in business, contracting out to skyscrapers in the big cities, and carpet cleaners followed suit. By the 1960s, companies were offering full-service cleaning—windows, carpets, and drapes. With downsizing in the 1980s, the services of independent cleaning companies replaced many of the custodial crews of large buildings. Better cleaning products have also helped the industry; more powerful machines and cleaning formulas have made work easier and quicker than in the days of waxes and polishes.

The Job

Ever try to get a Kool-Aid stain out of the sofa? Or try lugging a rented rug shampoo machine into your house for a cleaning? Then you have an idea of the demands of a cleaning service. People hire cleaning services to remove dirt and stubborn stains from the carpets in their homes. Cleaners come to your house with their own equipment and chemicals to wash the rugs and vacuum them. They take down drapes, clean them, then rehang them. They restore and refinish hardwood floors. With special high-powered vacuums and brushes, they clean air ducts. In addition to working in homes, they also clean offices and other large public buildings.

To become "The Best Swedish Carpet Cleaner in Phoenix," as his promotions claim, Anders Berg has been building his business for the last 10 years. "It can be feast or famine," he says. "There may be many jobs one day, and none another. But I keep fairly well booked; I have two to three jobs a day throughout the week." He starts his day at around 7:30 AM, making phone calls to confirm jobs for the day. In addition to carpet cleaning, Anders offers clients carpet dyeing, upholstery cleaning, duct cleaning, vacuum sales and repair, water and flood restoration, and many other services. He works weekends, holidays, and six-day work weeks. "It's a service business," he says, "so, when you're needed, you respond."

Carpet cleaners use different methods and equipment. For hot water extraction, a hot-water cleaning solution is first sprayed on the carpet. The soil dissolves in the solution, and the solution is then lifted from the carpet with a wet vacuum. Although it's commonly known as "steam" cleaning, no steam is actually generated by the heated solution. Shampooing is another method: it involves applying the cleaning solution to the carpet with a circular brush. The brush spins, rubbing the carpet and frothing the solution into a foam. The soil is then suspended and removed by wet/dry vacuuming. Other methods of carpet cleaning are foam cleaning and dry cleaning.

To clean the carpets of his clients, Anders owns a service truck and a cleaning machine. "Maintaining equipment can be costly," he says. He must also visit a supplier once a week for the chemicals he needs. When dealing with flood and water damage, he uses deodorizers and sanitizers and may have to rent additional equipment for the job.

Some cleaning services specialize in disaster restoration. After a house or building has been damaged by fire, smoke, or flooding, restorers are brought in to clean. With special skills, they work to restore the property to its original state, cleaning and repairing from top to bottom. Walls, ceilings, carpets, and furniture are cleaned. Carpets may be extracted and deodorized. Damaged furniture is reupholstered. Some companies even repair damaged books, documents, electronics, diskettes, and microfilm. Cleaning services that offer restoration often maintain a 24-hour phone number for emergencies.

A cleaning service may contract with a company to clean offices and apartments on a regular basis. They perform the usual cleaning of carpets and drapes and also fire-retard drapes to meet local fire ordinances. They clean fabric walls and fabric partitions. Cleaning services usually only enter office buildings after business hours, so commercial work often involves late evenings and weekends.

"Residential carpet cleaning is nice," Anders says. "You meet different people every day. And most people are appreciative." Anders must regularly promote his services to build up a client base. "I always have to look for new clients," he says, "and try to keep the ones I have. Once upon a time, a CPA would hang out his shingle, and before he knew it, he had clients. It's a more complicated process now. There's more competition." When you're running your own cleaning service, you must also attend to your own administrative concerns, such as scheduling, bookkeeping, and billing.

Requirements

High School

Because the materials, chemicals, and equipment for professional cleaning are likely to become more complicated, you should take courses that will help you adapt to chemical and mechanical advancements. Science courses can teach you about the products you'll be using. You'll be purchasing and using your own equipment, so a vocational class that involves you in mechanics can help you better understand the machines and their repair. Accounting classes and student business organizations will prepare you for the record-keeping aspect of the work. Take English and composition courses to develop writing skills for your own advertising and promotion.

Postsecondary Training

Though this may change in the near future, the cleaning services industry had been typically easy to break into. If you're looking for employment with a cleaning service, you probably won't need any special certification, or even a high school diploma. Even as you develop your own service, you probably won't be hindered by a lack of education or training when seeking clients. As the job becomes more technically demanding, however, training programs will become standard.

Kenway Mead, executive administrator for the Institute of Inspection Cleaning and Restoration Certification (IICRC), advises students to get firsthand experience in the business. You should seek out large cleaning businesses that contract their services to companies; these larger companies will be more likely to have good training systems in place. You should look for a company that has some certification and belongs to either regional or national professional organizations. Membership with such an organization will mean the company is privy to training information and requirements.

The IICRC offers seminars and conferences, as does the Association of Specialists in Cleaning and Restoration (ASCR). Some technical schools and community colleges offer training for cleaning technicians seeking certification. These schools offer courses in the use and care of cleaning agents, supplies, and equipment, as well as job organization and planning.

Certification or Licensing

Certification isn't required to run a cleaning service, but it can help you attract business. You should either belong to a regional professional association or seek certification with the IICRC or the ASCR. Several different categories of certification are available, including carpet cleaning technician, commercial carpet maintenance technician, and upholstery and fabric cleaning technician. The ASCR offers certification for disaster restoration. Because of the special skills required for removing smoke and water from property, restoration certification involves a demanding program of training and testing. Approximately 15 percent of cleaning service workers are certified.

Other Requirements

"I'm an obsessive-compulsive cleaner," Anders says. "That's not my natural language, but I noticed that phrase in someone's profile, and thought it was a really good description. I'm a clean freak." In addition to a love for cleaning, you should also have a talent for it. "In baseball," Anders says, "when a guy doesn't swing [at a ball out of the strike zone], he has a good eye. That's what most people lack in cleaning. People don't vacuum in an organized way. The smarter, more efficiently you work, the less time you spend on the task." You also need good business sense and the ability to constantly promote and market your business. You should be friendly with your customers to encourage repeat business.

Exploring

There's no shortage of opportunities for you to test your interest in cleaning. Many different organizations in your community need volunteers for such work. The social services department that assists the elderly and the disabled in your town relies on volunteers and part-time workers to go into homes and clean for those who can't do it themselves. Those jobs will generally involve only light cleaning and vacuuming. Because most of your work will involve solutions and equipment, rent a carpet cleaning machine and try it out. Clean all the carpets in your house, and you'll get a sense of the daily duties of a cleaning service owner (though professional cleaning tools are often larger and more complex than the ones you rent from a store). Large cleaning services that clean office buildings and stores often hire high school students for evening hours and weekends. Working even part-time, you'll learn a lot about the cleaning equipment and requirements of the work.

Employers

Many cleaning services are one-owner operations, but some may hire 40 or more people to assist with corporate contracts or disaster restoration. If you're in business for yourself, you may offer both commercial service and residential service, but you're likely to want to choose between the two. If contracted for commercial service (cleaning an office building, a mall, an apartment building, or some other public area), you'll probably sign on for a number of months with a predetermined number of cleanings per week. Working the residential market will involve working with different clients every day.

Starting Out

A lot of people who own cleaning services started their own businesses after working in other jobs. With the downsizing of the 1980s, many members of corporate cleaning crews started their own commercial cleaning services after being laid off. Anders has worked in some aspect of the cleaning industry since 1969, mostly in sales and consulting positions. "I had done some carpet cleaning in Sweden," he says. "But it's not as common there. People usually just threw their carpet out." When he moved to Phoenix, a friend suggested he start his own service, which he has now had for 10 years.

Start-up costs are relatively low. Depending on the kind of work you'll be doing, the initial expense of your equipment is likely to be much less than $4,000 (not including the van or truck needed for transporting the equipment).

Advancement

Once you've established your own business, you'll have to work hard to maintain a customer base and promote your services to expand your clientele. As you gain experience and make connections, you'll be able to expand your business into other areas. Some cleaning services sell cleaning products and vacuums, sell and install new carpet, and offer landscaping and maintenance services. Taking on a number of commercial contracts can mean big money, but it also requires a complete staff. Disaster restoration work for commercial properties can earn millions of dollars for a good, certified restoration service that has the special equipment and a staff of highly skilled technicians.

Earnings

Because of the differing sizes of cleaning services, from franchises and one-owner operations, to multi-million dollar cleaning companies, few accurate salary statistics have been compiled. Kenway Mead of the IICRC estimates that a carpet cleaning technician working for a service makes between $8 and $12 per hour, while a hard-working entrepreneur with a single-person operation can make between $42,000 and $60,000 a year. Someone with a disaster restoration service can make a lot more money from contracts with insurance companies, but it's also a lot more work, requiring more staff.

A carpet cleaner providing residential service will charge per room, per hour, or per square foot. Services charge between $20 and $50 per room, with extra charges for disinfectant and fabric protection. To clean upholstery, a cleaner will charge between $30 and $50 for each piece of furniture.

Work Environment

You'll be working with heavy equipment and chemicals that you may be sensitive to. "It's a lot of physical work," Anders says, "and it can be repetitive. You can wear out your legs, your arms, your back." The equipment and vacuums can be noisy. With the exception of hauling your equipment from your truck to the home or building, your work will be primarily inside. If in business for yourself, you won't have any supervision beyond the comments and opinions of your clientele. In most cases, you'll be allowed to work alone in the homes and in unoccupied commercial properties. Most of your work will be routine, but if you also provide disaster restoration, you'll be working in flooded or fire-damaged homes and buildings. With larger projects, you may be working with a team of cleaners and restorers.

Cleaning service owners average 40 hours or more per week. They often work weekends, holidays, and after business hours and occasionally deal with late-night restoration emergencies. When not actually cleaning, owners must devote time to equipment maintenance, record-keeping, and calling clients.

Outlook

The demand for cleaning services has grown steadily over the last 20 years, and should continue to do so. Office buildings make up the biggest share of the cleaning services market, but the marketplace is expanding to include more government buildings and industrial plants. Cleaning services were listed as one of the best "evergreen businesses" (consistently profitable businesses) in a ranking of home businesses by *Working at Home Magazine*.

Kenway Mead of IICRC predicts that the business will become more scientific, requiring a more intensive education. He also anticipates that environmental concerns will mean more business for cleaning services. "Cleaning affects indoor air quality," he points out. The ASCR sponsors research into the testing of products, cleaning methods, and toxicity. Less chemical-based cleaning methods are currently in development.

As the science of cleaning advances, more specialization within the market will be required. In order to best understand your equipment, methods, and solutions, you may need to narrow your services to residential, commercial, or restoration. Restorers who service large businesses will have to keep up with the technology of electronics and information storage in order to best restore office hardware and software.

For More Information

For career information, cleaning facts, and more, visit ASCR's Web site.

Association of Specialists in Cleaning and Restoration (ASCR)
8229 Cloverleaf Drive, Suite 460
Millersville, MD 21108
Tel: 800-272-7012
Web: http://www.ascr.org

For certification information, contact:

Institute of Inspection Cleaning and Restoration Certification (IICRC)
2715 East Mill Plain Boulevard
Vancouver, WA 98661
Tel: 360-693-5675
Web: http://www.iicrc.org

Computer Support Service Owners

Business **Computer science** **Technical/Shop**	School Subjects
Helping/teaching **Technical/scientific**	Personal Skills
Primarily multiple locations **Primarily indoors**	Work Environment
Associate's degree	Minimum Education Level
$35,000 to $62,000 to $150,000+	Salary Range
Voluntary	Certification or Licensing
Much faster than the average	Outlook

Overview

The owners of computer support services help businesses and individuals install and maintain computer hardware and software. They offer advice on what computers to purchase; they teach how to use the computers; and they assist with computer problems as they arise. There are close to 100,000 computer support people in the industry, including technicians and entrepreneurs. *Computer consultants* either work out of their homes, or they rent office space. Though some of their assistance is offered over the phone, much of their work is performed on-site.

History

Did you know there are museums devoted to "antique" computer hardware? Hang on to those old monitors, keyboards, and hard drives—they may be worth something to collectors and archivists some day. But when you think about computers, you're probably not thinking about the past. Computer hardware and software is most often talked about in terms of the future, but computer technology has been in development for over a century. In 1854, George Boole (1815-64) invented Boolean Algebra, a symbol and logic system used as the basis of computer design.

The 1950s brought IBM's first computers and the computer programming languages COBOL and LISP. By the late 1960s, people with computer skills served as consultants to manufacturers in the development of hardware and software. The Independent Computer Consultants Association (ICCA) was founded in 1976. Consultants had many more opportunities when even small businesses began investing in computers. Office software like spreadsheet programs and programs that link computers together with a shared hard drive were developed in the early 1980s. Many businesses and schools required the regular services of computer support technicians by the late 1980s.

The Job

If your computer's not working, the problem may be simply that you've forgotten to plug in the machine. But it can be much more complicated than that, requiring the assistance of someone with a great deal of computer knowledge. Today's hardware and software are easier to use than in previous years, but can be difficult to install correctly and difficult to learn. If you own a computer support service, you'll use your computer expertise to help businesses and individuals buy new computers and ready them for daily use.

With your operations based in your home office, you'll take calls from new clients, as well as clients who regularly rely on your services. Clients may have problems with their printers not responding to computer commands; a computer may be locked up; they may have problems performing the particular functions their software is designed for. In some cases, you'll be able to diagnose the problem and offer assistance over the phone. But in most cases, you'll be required to go to the offices and work hands-on with the computer systems. Armed with a cell phone, pager, and laptop, you'll drive to the offices of businesses small and large and the homes of personal computer owners to help get the computers running again. You will install network systems and new hardware and software. You'll upgrade existing systems. You'll also teach the computer operators, either one on one or in group training sessions, how to use the new systems. You can advise in the purchase of hardware and software, and prepare backup methods.

Many computer consultants also offer their expertise in Web design and multimedia for uploading a Web page, preparing a presentation, and offering desktop publishing services. They also help to create computer databases. Some computer consultants are involved in issues of programming. The Year 2000 problem (Y2K) has required consultants to have a knowledge of the solutions available to businesses.

Brad Crotteau started his own computer support service in 1991, and his business has grown into Crocker Networking Solutions, Inc. He anticipated that some of the demands of the job would become more difficult as he got older, so he recently made some decisions about the nature of his business. "I knew I didn't always want to be crawling around, plugging computers in," he says. So Brad incorporated his business and took on a staff of nine employees, including technicians, sales people, administrative assistants, trainers, and Web designers.

Brad's day starts early at 7:00 AM with paperwork, followed at around 8:00 AM by phone calls from businesses. He then must work the new requests for service into his daily schedule. Though he has a staff of nine, Brad is still actively involved in the technical work of installing systems and troubleshooting, and the generating of estimates and other financial details. He makes it a point to end his work day at 6:00 PM, though he is required to work some overtime. "I have stayed up until 4:00 AM," he says, "bringing a service up for a client, but that's rare." His client base consists of businesses with between 5 and 85 personal computers. The biggest challenge can be correcting user-generated problems. Brad says giving an inexperienced computer user a complex system "is like giving a Maserati to someone who just started riding horses a few weeks ago."

Brad's support service is also embarking on a new business venture. He has trademarked many of his company's services, and now offers them as a product called "Performance Net." His company sells the network systems, then puts the systems into place. This venture has been helped along by a business alliance with a manufacturer of software. Brad's company has been hired by the manufacturer to install their servers in businesses all across the country.

In addition to the technical work, the owners of computer support services must handle all the details of running their businesses. They handle phone calls, bookkeeping, and client records. They must also research new technologies and keep up to date on advanced technical skills. Maintaining connections within the industry is also important; you may need to call upon the assistance of other consultants and technicians to help with some projects.

Requirements

High School

Of course, you should take any classes that will familiarize you with computers. Computer science classes will help you learn about operating systems and programming. Learn about the various software, like word processing and spreadsheet programs, as well as the languages of Internet Web page design. A journalism class, and working on your school newspaper, will involve you with multimedia presentation and teach you about page layout and graphic design. Take courses in business and accounting to prepare for the bookkeeping and administrative details of the work. English composition and communication courses can help you develop teaching skills.

Postsecondary Training

Though a degree isn't required for you to start your own computer support service, most service owners and consultants have at least an associate's degree. Some consultants supplement their education with special training offered by computer software companies such as Novell and Microsoft. Many consultants registered with the ICCA have advanced degrees and highly technical training in such areas as robotics, telecommunications, and nuclear engineering. Community colleges and universities across the country have programs in computer science, computer engineering, and electrical engineering. For a degree in computer science, you'll be required to take courses in calculus, English composition, program design, algorithms, computer graphics, and database management. Electrical engineering programs include courses in BASIC programming, industrial electronics, digital integrated circuits, and microprocessor systems. In addition to seminars, you'll also attend labs. Some bachelor's programs include research projects in which you'll work closely with a faculty member in studying new technologies. Some software companies offer training programs.

Very few consultants start their own businesses straight out of college. Some years working full-time as part of a computer service staff will give you the firsthand experience you'll need. Not only will you develop your computer expertise, but you'll learn what's required in operating a business.

Certification or Licensing

There are many different kinds of certifications available to people working in computer support and consulting. No one certification, however, serves all the varying needs of computer professionals. Some consultants get certified in database design and administration. Some consultants have Microsoft Certified System Engineer (MCSE) status. The Association of Computer Support Specialists (ACSS) offers online training courses for the MCSE exam, which tests your understanding of Windows 98 networks, hardware requirements and installations, and system maintenance. This certification should only supplement an extensive computer background, not replace it. The term "paper MCSE" has evolved in the industry to describe those who "look good on paper" with their certification, but don't have the networking and computer science education and experience to back it up.

The Institute for Certification of Computer Professionals (ICCP) offers a Certified Computer Professional (CCP) exam. Around 50,000 computer professionals hold the certification, having passed an exam that tests knowledge of business information systems, data resource management, software engineering, and other subjects.

Other Requirements

You should have good business and money management skills. Though some months you may have more work than you can handle, with a steady flow of income, other months there may be no work at all. You'll have to budget your money to carry you through the lean months. Though computer skills are very important, you can't be a computer "geek"—you'll need good people skills to maintain customer relations.

Teaching skills are important, as you'll be training people in how to use their systems. "You need the ability to talk to people in a language they can understand," Brad says, "but don't talk down to them. You have to gauge your client's understanding."

Exploring

Get to know your own home computer—study the software and its manuals, and familiarize yourself with computer programming languages. Read some of the many magazines devoted to computers, such as *MacWorld* and *PC Today*. Find out who services the computers in your school, and ask to spend some time with the technicians. But don't just focus on the technical duties of the people who own computer support services; find out how they go about running an office and maintaining a small business. Join your school's business club and you'll have the opportunity to meet small business owners in your area.

Employers

You'll be working for a variety of different clients, servicing the personal computers in home-based offices, as well as contracting with large companies for long-term assistance. Though many individuals have computers in their homes for their personal use, few of them seek out professional service. Your main clients will be accounting firms, insurance agencies, government departments—any business or organization that relies upon computers to perform daily operations. Even a company that has its own full-time support staff will occasionally hire outside consultants. Computer support services are in demand all across the country, but are most successful in large cities where they can draw from a broader client base.

Starting Out

Brad had been working for Pacific Gas and Electric as an engineer for 14 years when he began developing his own business on the side. "The main concern for people starting their own businesses," Brad says, "is how they're going to capitalize their company." Brad was fortunate to receive an early retirement package, then worked for a while as a computer consultant for a private consulting company. Once he'd felt he'd gotten his feet wet, he was ready to start full-time with his own support service. "You should work for a large corporation," Brad advises, "to learn about human resources, compensation packages, benefits. You need to develop a good business sense. That's why many small businesses fail—you may be great at computers, but bad at business."

As with many start-ups, it's good for you to focus your talents. Decide on a niche, such as networking, or package customization, then promote those specific services. Brad credits much of his success to good marketing techniques, which includes careful attention to image. "You can't do this from the back of your car," he says, "but promoting a good image doesn't have to be expensive. Our biggest sales tool is our business cards. We have a nice, multicolored business card that reads well."

Advancement

Once you've established yourself in your niche market, you can expand to include other services. Some computer support services are able to offer much more than technical assistance; they also hold training sessions, prepare multimedia reports and presentations, and design Web pages. The more business connections you make with support services, computer manufacturers, and other companies, the better you'll be able to build your client base. As your business grows, you can hire staff to deal with administrative duties, as well as technicians to assist with servicing your clients' computers. With the proper office space, you can conduct training sessions in various software programs and the Internet.

Earnings

A number of interactive salary surveys have been conducted for computer consultants, and are posted at http://www.realrates.com, http://www.computerjobs.com, http://www.pencomsi.com, and other company Web sites. These surveys show a wide salary range, but estimate the median annual earnings for computer consultants at $55,000 to $65,000. In the first few years of a business, a consultant will make about $40,000 or less, depending on location. Those working in large cities like New York and Los Angeles average more than those in the Midwest, the Southwest, and the Northwest. Someone in New York with more than 10 years experience will average over $90,000 a year, while a consultant with similar experience in the Southwest may make around $65,000 a year. Some very experienced, business-minded consultants can make $150,000 a year or more.

Work Environment

If you're running your business entirely by yourself, the base of your operations will be a home office, or a rented commercial space. You'll devote a lot of time to sitting at your own computer, managing your accounts and records, but the majority of your time will be in the offices of your clients. In either case, your environment will likely be quiet and well lit. When installing and repairing computer hardware, you may have to do some crawling around behind desks to hook up wires and plug in cords. Your work is essentially unsupervised, but some clients may stay close at your side for instruction as you fix their computer problems. In some cases, you may be working as part of a team, particularly if you're brought into a large company with a full-time support staff. Your work will be indoors, though you'll be traveling from office to office throughout the day.

Some consultants work much more than 40 hours a week, though you can avoid the long hours with a well-managed business. "If you're working 80 hours a week," Brad says, "something's wrong. You'll have to work hard, but you don't have to obsess about it."

Outlook

The industry is expected to grow quickly as computer systems become more important to more businesses. Lower prices on computer hardware and software will inspire businesses to expand their systems, and to invest in the services needed to keep them up and running. Computers will also become more sophisticated, and will be able to perform more complex operations; consultants will be needed to help people understand these new, complicated computer programs. With companies relying more on complex computer systems, they'll be less likely to take risks in the installation of hardware and software. *Working at Home* magazine lists computer consulting as the best high-tech home business. To stay at the top of the industry, consultants will have to keep up on technological developments and take continuing education courses.

More consultants may also become involved in broadening computer literacy. Computer resources are generally limited to middle class students; some nonprofit organizations are forming to bring more computers and support services to inner-city youth, low-income families, and people with disabilities.

For More Information

To subscribe to a free electronic newsletter, and to check out an extensive list of related Web links, visit the ACSS Web page. You can also write to them to learn more about membership and their career training courses.

Association of Computer Support Specialists (ACSS)
218 Huntington Road
Bridgeport, CT 06608
Tel: 203-332-1524
Web: http://www.acss.org

To learn about membership benefits of the ICCA, contact:

Independent Computer Consultants Association (ICCA)
11131 South Towne Square, Suite F
St. Louis, MO 63123
Tel: 800-774-4222
Web: http://www.icca.org

To obtain a free Salary, Reference and Advice guide for technology managers and computer consultants, contact:

RHI Consulting-Technology Professionals
Web: http://www.rhic.com

Desktop Publishing Specialists

Art Computer science English	School Subjects
Artistic Communication/ideas	Personal Skills
Primarily one location Primarily indoors	Work Environment
$18,000 to $30,000 to $83,000	Salary Range
Voluntary	Certification or Licensing
Faster than the average	Outlook

Overview

Desktop publishing specialists prepare reports, brochures, books, cards, and other documents for printing. They create computer files of text, graphics, and page layout. They work with files others have created, or they compose original text and graphics for the client. There are around 50,000 desktop publishing specialists working in the printing industry, either as freelancers or for corporations, service bureaus, and advertising agencies.

History

When Johannes Gutenberg (1400?-1468?), way back in the 1440s, invented movable type, it seemed like a major technological advancement. Up until that point, books were produced entirely by hand by monks, every word written in ink on vellum. Though print shops flourished all across Europe with this invention, inspiring the production of millions of books by the 1500s, there was no other major change in the technology of printing until the 1800s. By then, cylinder presses were churning out thousands of sheets per hour, and the Linotype machine allowed for easier, more efficient plate-making. Offset lithography (a method of applying ink from a treated surface onto paper) followed and gained popularity after World War II. Phototypesetting was later developed, involving creating film images of text and pictures to be printed. At the end of the 20th century, computers caused another revolution in the industry. Laser printers now allow for low-cost, high-quality printing, and desktop publishing software is credited with spurring sales and use of personal home computers.

The Job

If you've ever used a computer to design and print flyers to promote a high school play, or if you've put together a small literary magazine, then you've had some experience in desktop publishing. Not so many years ago, the pre-press process (the steps to prepare a document for the printing press) involved metal casts, molten lead, light tables, knives, wax, paste, and a number of different professionals from artists to typesetters. With computer technology, these jobs are becoming more consolidated. A desktop publishing specialist is someone with artistic talents, proofreading skills, sales and marketing abilities, and a great deal of computer knowledge. As a desktop publishing specialist, you'll work on computers converting and preparing files for printing presses and other media, such as the Internet and CD-ROM. Much of desktop publishing fits into the prepress category, and desktop publishing specialists typeset, or arrange and transform, text and graphics. Your work is performed at a home computer using the latest in design software. Macintosh programs such as FreeHand, Illustrator, and PageMaker, are the most popular with desktop publishing specialists, though PC programs like Corel Draw and PhotoShop are also gaining popularity. Some desktop publishing specialists use CAD (computer-aided design) technology, allowing them to create images and effects with a digitizing pen.

Once you've created the file to be printed, you'll either submit it to a commercial printer, or you'll print the pieces yourself. Whereas traditional typesetting costs over $20 per page, desktop printing can cost less than a penny a page. Individuals hire the services of desktop publishing specialists for creating and printing invitations, advertising and fundraising brochures, newsletters, flyers, and business cards. Commercial printing involves catalogs, brochures, and reports, while business printing encompasses products used by businesses, such as sales receipts and forms.

Typesetting and page layout work entails selecting font types and sizes, arranging column widths, checking for proper spacing between letters, words, and columns, placing graphics and pictures, and more. You'll choose from the hundreds of typefaces available, taking the purpose and tone of the text into consideration when selecting from fonts with round shapes or long shapes, thick strokes or thin, serifs or sans serifs. Editing is also an important duty of a desktop publishing specialist. Articles must be updated, or in some cases rewritten, before they be arranged on a page. As more people use their own desktop publishing programs to create print-ready files, you'll have to be skillful at designing original work, and promoting your talents, in order to remain competitive.

Darryl Gabriel and his wife Maree own a desktop publishing service in Australia—the Internet has allowed them to publicize the business globally. They currently serve customers in their local area and across Australia, and are hoping to expand more into international Internet marketing. Darryl and Maree use a computer ("But one is not enough," Darryl says), a laser printer, and a scanner to create business cards, pamphlets, labels, books, and personalized greeting cards. Though they must maintain computer skills, they also have a practical understanding of the equipment. "We keep our prices down by being able to re-ink our cartridges," Darryl says. "This takes a little getting used to at first, but once you get a knack for it, it becomes easier."

You'll be dealing with technical issues, such as resolution problems, colors that need to be corrected, and software difficulties, but you'll also use creativity and artistic skills to create designs. Many of your clients will bring you graphics they've designed themselves using computer software programs, while others will bring you drawings in pencil and paper. They provide you with their designs, and you must convert these designs to the format requested by the designers. A designer may come in with a hand-drawn sketch, a printout of a design, or a file on a diskette, and he or she may want the design to be ready for publication on the World Wide Web, in a high-quality brochure, or in a newspaper or magazine. Each format presents different issues, and you must be familiar with the processes and solutions for each. You may also provide services such as color scanning, laminating, image manipulation, and poster production.

Customer relations are as important as technical skills. Darryl emphasizes the importance of learning how to use your equipment and software to their fullest potential, but he also advises you to know your customers. "Try and be as helpful as possible to your customers," he says, "so you can provide them with products that they are happy with and that are going to benefit their businesses." He says it's also very important to follow up, calling customers to make sure they're pleased with the work. "If you're able to relate to what the customers want, and if you encourage them to be involved in the initial design process, then they'll be confident they're going to get quality products."

Requirements

High School

Classes that will help you develop desktop publishing skills include computer classes and design and art classes. Computer classes should include both hardware and software, since understanding how computers function will help you with troubleshooting and knowing the computer's limits. In photography classes you can learn about composition, color, and design elements. Typing, drafting, and print shop classes, if available, will also provide you with the opportunity to gain some indispensable skills. Working on the school newspaper or yearbook will train you on desktop publishing skills as well, including page layout, typesetting, composition, and working under a deadline.

Postsecondary Training

Although a college degree is not a prerequisite, many desktop publishing specialists have at least a bachelor's degree. Areas of study range anywhere from English and communications, to graphic design. Some two-year colleges and technical institutes offer programs in desktop publishing or related fields. A growing number of schools offer programs in technical and visual communications, which may include classes in desktop publishing, layout and design, and computer graphics. Four-year colleges also offer courses in technical communications and graphic design. There are many opportunities to take classes related to desktop publishing through extended education programs offered through universities and colleges. These classes can range from basic desktop publishing techniques to advanced courses in Adobe Photoshop or QuarkXPress and are often taught by professionals working in the industry.

A number of professional organizations and schools offer scholarship and grant opportunities. The Graphic Arts Education and Research Foundation (GAERF) and the Education Council of the Graphic Arts Industry, Inc., both divisions of the Association for Suppliers of Printing and Publishing Technologies (NPES), can provide information on scholarship opportunities and research grants. Other organizations that offer financial awards and information on scholarship opportunities include the Society for Technical Communication, the International Prepress Association, the Printing Industries of America (PIA), and the Graphic Arts Technical Foundation, which offers scholarships in graphic communications through the National Scholarship Trust Fund.

Certification or Licensing

Certification is not mandatory, and currently there is only one certification program offered in desktop publishing. The Association of Graphic Communications has an Electronic Publishing Certificate designed to set industry standards and measure the competency levels of desktop publishing specialists. The examination is divided into a written portion and a hands-on portion. During the practical portion of the examination, candidates receive files on a disk and must manipulate images and text, make color corrections, and perform whatever tasks are necessary to create the final product. Applicants are expected to be knowledgeable in print production, color separation, typography and font management, computer hardware and software, image manipulation, page layout, scanning and color correcting, prepress and preflighting, and output device capabilities.

PIA is in the process of developing industry standards in the prepress and press industries. PIA may eventually design a certification program in desktop publishing or electronic prepress operation.

Other Requirements

Desktop publishing specialists are detail-oriented, possess problem-solving skills, and have a sense of design and artistic skills. "People tell me I have a flair for graphic design," Darryl says, "and mixing the right color with the right graphics." A good eye and patience are critical, as well as endurance to see projects through to the finish. You should have an aptitude for computers, the ability to type quickly and accurately, and a natural curiosity. A calm temperament comes in handy when working under pressure and constant deadlines. You should be flexible and be able to handle more than one project at a time.

Exploring

Experimenting with your home computer, or a computer at school or the library, will give you a good idea as to whether desktop publishing is for you. Play around with various graphic design and page layout programs. If you subscribe to an Internet service, take advantage of any free Web space available to you and design your own home page. Join computer clubs and volunteer at small organizations to produce newsletters and flyers; volunteering is an excellent way to try new software and techniques, and to gain experience troubleshooting and creating final products. Also, part-time or summer employment with printing shops and companies that have in-house publishing or printing departments are great ways to gain experience and make valuable contacts.

Employers

Your clients will include individuals and small business owners, such as publishing houses, advertising agencies, graphic design agencies, and printing shops. Some large companies also contract with desktop publishing services, rather than hire full-time staffs of designers. Government agencies hire desktop publishing specialists for the large number of documents they publish. The Government Printing Office (GPO) has a Digital Information Technology Support Group (DITS Group) that provides desktop and electronic publishing services to federal agencies.

You'll usually be dealing directly with your clients, but in some cases you may be subcontracting work from printers, designers, and other desktop publishing specialists. You may also hire your services as a consultant, working with printing professionals to help solve particular design problems.

Starting Out

To start your own business, you must have a great deal of experience with design and page layout, and a careful understanding of the computer design programs you'll be using. Before striking out on your own, you may want to gain experience as a full-time staff member of a large business. Most desktop publishing specialists enter the field through the production side, or the editorial side of the industry. Those with training as a designer or artist can easily master the finer techniques of production. Printing houses and design agencies are places to check for production artist opportunities. Publishing companies often hire desktop publishing specialists to work in-house or as freelance employees. Working within the industry, you can make connections and build up a clientele.

You can also start out by investing in computer hardware and software, and volunteering your services. By designing logos, letterhead, and restaurant menus, your work will gain quick recognition, and word of your services will spread.

Advancement

The growth of Darryl and Maree's business is requiring that they invest in another computer and printer. "We want to expand," Darryl says, "develop with technology, and venture into Internet marketing and development. We also intend to be a thorn in the side of the larger commercial printing businesses in town." In addition to taking on more print projects, you can expand your business into Web design and page layout for Internet magazines.

Earnings

There is limited salary information available for desktop publishing specialists, most likely because the job duties of desktop publishing specialists can vary and often overlap with other jobs. According to a salary survey conducted by PIA in 1997, the average wage of desktop publishing specialists in the prepress department ranged from $11.72 to $14.65 an hour, with the highest rate at $40 an hour. Entry-level desktop publishing specialists with little or no experience generally earn minimum wage. Electronic page make-up system operators earned an average of $13.62 to $16.96, and scanner operators ranged from $14.89 to $17.91.

According to the *1998-99 Occupational Outlook Handbook*, full-time pre-press workers in typesetting and composition earned a median wage of $421 a week, or $21,892 annually. Wage rates vary depending on experience, training, region, and size of the company.

Work Environment

Desktop publishing specialists spend most of their time working in front of a computer, whether editing text, or laying out pages. They need to be able to work with other prepress operators, and deal with clients. Hours may vary depending on project deadlines at hand. Some projects may take one day to complete, while others may take a week or longer. Projects may range from designing a logo for letterhead, preparing a catalog for the printer, or working on a file that will be published on the World Wide Web.

Outlook

According to the *1998-99 Occupational Outlook Handbook,* the field of desktop publishing is projected to be one of the fastest growing occupations, increasing about 75 percent through the year 2006. In 1996, there were a total of 30,000 desktop publishing specialists employed in the United States. As technology advances, the ability to create and publish documents will become easier and faster, thus influencing more businesses to produce printed materials. Desktop publishing specialists will be needed to satisfy typesetting, page layout, design, and editorial demands. With new equipment, commercial printing shops will be able to shorten the turnaround time on projects and in turn can increase business and accept more jobs. For instance, digital printing presses allow printing shops to print directly to the digital press rather than printing to a piece of film, and then printing from the film to the press. Digital printing presses eliminate an entire step and should appeal to companies who need jobs completed quickly.

According to a survey conducted by PIA in 1997, the printing industry is growing, which can be attributed partly to the growth experienced by the North American economy. The electronic prepress segment of the printing market enjoyed the most growth, with an average change from 1996 of 9.3 percent. Traditional prepress, on the other hand, suffered a decline of 5.7 percent. PIA's survey also indicates that printing firms have been experiencing difficulties finding new, qualified employees. This is a good sign for desktop publishing specialists with skills and experience.

QuarkXPress, Adobe PageMaker, Macromedia FreeHand, Adobe Illustrator, and Adobe Photoshop are some programs often used in desktop publishing. Specialists with experience in these and other software will be in demand.

For More Information

For career information, and information about scholarships and education, contact:

Association for Suppliers of Printing, Publishing, and Converting Technologies (NPES)
1899 Preston White Drive
Reston, VA 20191-4367
Tel: 703-264-7200
Email: npes@npes.org
Web: http://www.npes.org

For scholarship information, contact:

National Scholarship Trust Fund of the Graphic Arts
200 Deer Run Road
Sewickley, PA 15143-2600
Tel: 800-900-GATF
Email: info@gatf.org
Web: http://www.gatf.org

For career brochures and information about grants and scholarships, contact:

Society for Technical Communication
901 North Stuart Street, Suite 904
Arlington, VA 22203-1854
Tel: 703-522-4114
Web: http://www.stc-va.org

To obtain an issue of Desktop Publishers Journal, *a trade magazine for desktop publishers, contact:*

Desktop Publishers Journal

462 Boston Street
Topfield, MA 01983-1232
Tel: 978-887-7900
Web: http://www.dtpjournal.com

Independent Computer Consultants Association (ICCA)

11131 South Towne Square, Suite F
St. Louis, MO 63123
Tel: 800-774-4222
Web: http://www.icca.org

Florists

	School Subjects
Art Business	
	Personal Skills
Artistic Following instructions Leadership/management	
	Work Environment
Primarily indoors Primarily one location	
	Minimum Education Level
High school diploma	
	Salary Range
$4.25/hour to $8.39/hour to $17.00/hour	
	Certification or Licensing
Recommended	
	Outlook
Faster than the average	

Overview

Floral designers, or *florists,* arrange live or cut flowers, potted plants, foliage, or other decorative items, according to basic design principles to make eye pleasing creations. Designers make such arrangements for birthdays, weddings, funerals, or other occasions. They are employed by small local flower shops or larger national chains, grocery stores, or established at-home businesses. There are over 200,000 floral design workers employed in the United States.

History

Flowers have been used for centuries as decoration, personal adornment, or for religious significance. Ancient Egyptians used flowers to honor their many gods and goddesses. Flowers were arranged in low bowls in an orderly, repetitive pattern—flower, bud, foliage, and so on. Special spouted vases were also used to hold flowers. Lotus flowers, also called water lilies, were Egyptian favorites. They came to symbolize sacredness, and were associated with Isis, the Egyptian nature goddess. Flowers were sometimes used as decorations for the body, collar, and hair.

Flowers were fashioned into elaborate wreaths and garlands by the ancient Greeks. The best wreath makers were often commissioned by wealthy Greeks to make wreaths for gifts, awards, or for decoration. *Chaplets,* a special wreath for the head, were especially popular. *Cornucopia*, a horn shaped container still used today, was filled with arrangements of flowers, fruits, and vegetables. Flowers arranged into wreaths and garlands were also popular during the Roman Period and well through to the Middle Ages.

The Victorian Era saw great development in the art of floral design. There was enormous enthusiasm for flowers, plants, and gardens; the most cultured young ladies were often schooled in the art of flower arrangement. Rules were first established regarding function and design. Magazines and books about floral arrangement were also published during this time. Proper Victorian ladies often had fresh *nosegays,* or *tussie-mussies,* a hand-held arrangement of tightly knotted flowers, for sentimental reasons, if not to freshen the air. *Posy holders,* fancy carriers for these small floral arrangements, came into fashion. Some were made of ivory, glass, or mother-of-pearl, and were elaborately decorated with jewels or etchings. Flowers were also made into small arrangements and tucked into a lady's décolletage inside aptly named containers, *bosom bottles.*

Ikebana, the Japanese art of floral arrangement since the 6th century, has been a principal influence on formal flower arrangement design. Its popularity still continues today. In the 1950s, *Free Form Expression* developed, incorporating pieces of driftwood and figurines within arrangements of flowers and live plants.

Floral traditions of the past still have an impact on us today. It is still fashionable to mark special occasions with flowers, be it an anniversary, wedding, or birthday. People continue to use flowers to commemorate the dead. Today's floral arrangements reflect the current style, trends, and tastes. The best floral designers will follow the developing fashions and creatively adapt them to his or her arrangements.

The Job

From simple birthday bouquets to lavish wedding arrangements, floral designers define a sentiment, a mood, or make an impression, using flowers as their medium of expression. Along with live flowers, designers may use silk flowers or foliage, fresh fruit, twigs, or incorporate decorative items such as candles, balloons, ribbons, and stuffed animals to their arrangements. Good equipment—foam, wire, wooden or plastic picks, shears, florist's knife, tape, and a variety of containers—is essential. Techniques such as wiring flower stems, or shading the tips of blooms with paint or glitter, are often used to give floral arrangements a finished look. Familiarity with different species of flowers and plants, as well as creativity and knowledge of elements of design is what distinguishes a good floral designer from the ordinary.

Floral designers are fortunate to have a number of employment paths from which to choose. Some designers are employed at flower shops, while some opt to work independently. Aurora Gagni, proprietress of Floral Elegance, is one such entrepreneur. A registered nurse by training, but creative by nature, Aurora always enjoyed making crafts. "I would see a picture of a flower arrangement in a magazine, and try to duplicate it, but I would always add and experiment and make it my own creation." Aurora made floral arrangements, wreaths, and displays for family, friends, and coworkers, who in turn spread word of Aurora's abilities. "At one point, I found myself giving bow-making lessons at work!" In time, Aurora had a steady, and growing number of customers who relied on her skills.

What persuaded Aurora to give up nursing and go into business for herself? "My kids!" she answers. Indeed, this job perk is an attractive one, especially for someone juggling a career with family. Aurora conducts her business almost entirely from her home, and is available for the "many little things"—driving to and from sports events, delivering forgotten lunch boxes, and of course, homework.

Aurora tackles a variety of floral requests, but weddings are her specialty. While a typical wedding day lasts a few hours, the planning stage can take months. "Usually, the bride and groom look at my book," Aurora says, "and decide if they like my work." If so, the contract is "closed"—the contract agreement is signed, a budget is set, and a down payment is made—several months before the wedding day. Soon after, designs are made keeping the budget in mind. Many brides wish for orchids with a carnation budget. "I try to accommodate what type of flower, or color, or look the customer wants," Aurora explains, sometimes making alternate suggestions, especially if the price is an issue, or if the flower is difficult to obtain. Aurora orders necessary supplies weeks in advance and scouts for upcoming sales. She notifies her floral wholesalers in advance of any flowers that are seasonal or difficult to obtain. Also, she visits the church and reception hall to check on details such as size, location, and any restrictions. The quickest route to both destinations is also mapped out to ensure prompt delivery of the flowers.

Aurora periodically checks in with the bride about any last minute changes. Often times, more corsages or more banquet table centerpieces are needed to accommodate extra guests. Bows are tied and secured with wire about two weeks before the wedding. Three days before the wedding, flowers are picked and kept fresh in buckets of water treated with floral preservatives. The actual arranging, done in Aurora's basement, is begun the night before the wedding—bricks of floral foam, treated with water and preservatives, keep the flowers in place. Bouquets and corsages are delivered to the bride's home on the morning of the wedding and pew ribbons, flower arrangements, and corsages for the groom's part, are brought to the church. Aurora then goes to the hall to set up for the reception. Final touch-ups are given to table centerpieces, the head table is decorated, and the last of many details are tackled.

Aurora hires additional help for large contracts, especially to assist with the final arrangements. Her children also help when needed, and her husband is her unofficial delivery driver.

Most retail floral businesses keep a relatively small staff. Sales workers help customers place their orders; they also take care of phone orders. Drivers are hired to make deliveries. Sometimes assistant designers are employed.

Requirements

High School

Take art and design classes while in high school! After all, creativity is an important buzz word in this industry. Biology classes would be helpful in learning about plants and flowers. Do you have aspirations of owning a flower establishment? Sign up for business-related courses and computer classes—they will help make you a better entrepreneur.

Postsecondary Training

In the past, floral designers learned their craft on the job, usually working as an assistant or apprentice to an experienced designer. Most designers today, however, pursue advanced education and certification. Certification is not mandatory in this industry, but it does have some pull when applying for design positions. There are numerous universities that offer degrees in floriculture and horticulture, as well as community colleges and independent schools offering certification in floral design.

Programs vary from school to school, lasting anywhere from days to years depending on the type of degree or certification. The American Floral Art School, a state approved and licensed vocational school located in Chicago, Illinois, offers certification in modern floral design, with course schedules from one to three weeks. The curriculum includes the fundamentals of artistic floral design, general instruction in picking or wiring, tinting, and arranging flowers, different types of arrangements and their containers, fashion flowers and wedding flowers, and flower shop management.

Some schools, such as the Rittners School of Floral Design, based in Boston, Massachusetts, offer classes online. They also have a special seminar emphasizing floral business skills, a must if you plan on starting your own shop.

Other Requirements

Most people don't wake up one morning and decide to become a floral designer. If you don't have a creative and artistic inclination, you're already a step behind the rest. A good floral designer enjoys and understands plants and flowers, and can visualize a creation from the very first daffodil. Are you able to work well under pressure and deadlines, and effectively deal with vendors or wholesalers? These are daily requirements of the job. Also, be prepared to greet and accommodate all types of customers, from impatient grooms to nervous brides to grieving families. A compassionate and patient personality will help you go far in this field.

Exploring

Mulling a future in floral design? Now is the best time to determine if this career is the right one for you! As a high school student without experience, it's doubtful you'll be hired as a floral designer; but working as a cashier, flower delivery person, or an assistant are great ways to break into the industry.

What about taking some classes to test your talent? Michael's, a national arts and crafts retailer, offers floral design workshops—look for similar workshops in your area. Park district programs also have design classes, especially during the holiday seasons. Such programs are relatively inexpensive—most times the fee is just enough to cover materials used in class.

Learn the industry firsthand—why not spend a day at work with a floral designer? Explain your interest to your local florist (and promise to stay out of the way)!

Employers

According to *The Detroit News,* there are over 200,000 florists employed in the floral industry in the United States. Small, independently owned flower shops are the most common employers of florists. Large, national chains, such as Teleflora and FTD, supply additional jobs. Flower departments, now a staple in larger grocery stores, also employ floral designers.

Starting Out

Some floral designers get their start by working as assistant designers. Others, especially if they are certified, may be hired as floral designers. Experienced designers may concentrate in a certain area, such as weddings, and become wedding specialists.

Aurora needed to apply for a tax identification number before she officially "opened" her business. This number is necessary to establish accounts with wholesalers and greenhouses, as well as for tax purposes. It would be wise to consult with business or legal experts regarding income tax issues, promotion and advertising, and other matters dealing with operating your own business.

Professionals in floral design maintain a portfolio of their best designs. A portfolio is useful when applying for membership in floral association classes, and when wooing potential clients.

Advancement

Advancement in this field depends on the interest of the individual. Some floral designers are content to work at small local shops, especially if they have created a name for themselves in the area they serve. Others decide to try employment with larger national chains such as TeleFlora, or 1-800-

FLOWERS. Superstore grocery chains now boast full service floral departments, creating many job opportunities for designers.

Do you possess an entrepreneurial nature? Maybe owning a floral business—home-based or established in the middle of your town's business district—is in your future. Still other options include entering the field of landscape design; interior landscaping for offices, shopping centers and hotels; or a large floral design specialty. Imagine working on a float for Pasadena's Tournament of Roses Parade!

Many of Aurora's contracts are wedding related so it makes sense that her business branches out accordingly. Party favors, cake toppers, and the veil and cord—elements unique in many Latin wedding ceremonies—are some items Aurora customizes for her clients.

Earnings

Experience counts for a lot when it comes to a designer's salary. According to a 1997 salary survey conducted by *Floral Finance,* designers with one year of experience averaged $6.15 an hour, with a low of $4.25 and a high of $11.00. Those with three or more years of experience earned an average hourly of $8.39, ranging from $5.00 to $17.00. Manager/designers averaged about $10.35 an hour (low—$5.00; high—$25.00). Geographic location plays a part in salary differences as well. Floral designers on the East and West Coasts traditionally enjoy higher than average salaries, compared to other parts of the United States. However, this recent salary survey shows the Upper Midwest and Northwest areas had marked improvement. Stores located in large urban areas tend to have higher annual sales than those found in rural areas, resulting in higher pay for their employees.

Depending on the store, designers may be offered sick and vacation time, health and life insurance, as well as other benefits.

Work Environment

Flowers can be purchased almost anywhere, from small strip mall flower shops to large national chains to the neighborhood grocery store. This availability means that floral designers can work almost anywhere—from remote rural areas to busy cities.

Retail floral designers can expect to have comfortable work surroundings. Most floral shops are cool, clean, and well decorated to help attract customers. Glass refrigerators filled with fresh flowers, live plants and flower arrangements, and arts and crafts are typical items in any flower shop. Work stations for making floral pieces are usually found in the back of the store, along with supplies, containers, and necessary equipment.

Expect to spend the majority of the time on your feet—either standing while working on an arrangement, consulting with customers regarding types of flowers, or on a flower buying expedition. Most retail-based designers work a normal eight-hour work day with a day off during the week. Weekends are especially busy (think weddings) and holidays notoriously so. Christmas, Mother's Day, and Valentine's Day are peak times for floral orders. Long work hours are the norm during these times to accommodate the heavy demand for flowers.

Most designers, if contracted to work a wedding, will travel to the church or the banquet hall to make sure the church arrangements or the table arrangements are properly set up.

Outlook

The future for floral designers looks bright as a daisy. The field of design, floral design included, is expected to grow faster than the average for all other occupations through the year 2006, according to the U.S. Department of Labor. At least one flower shop is situated in even the smallest of towns. The emergence of full service floral departments in grocery stores, as well as international floral wire services such as Amlings, FTD, and TeleFlora, contributes to job availability. Floral experts who are able to create exciting and original designs will be in high demand. Certified designers may have an edge for the best jobs.

A growing population with large disposable incomes is good news for this industry. Sending flowers to mark an occasion is an old tradition that still has impact today. However, advancement in this career is limited unless you choose to enter management or open a business. Also, starting hourly pay for floral designers is considerably lower than in other design fields.

For More Information

For education and certification information, contact:

Society of American Florists
1601 Duke Street
Alexandria, VA 22314
Tel: 703-836-8700
Web: http://www.safnow.org/

For membership information, contact:

American Institute of Floral Designers
720 Light Street
Baltimore, MD 21230-3816
Tel: 410-752-3318
Email: aifd@assnhqtrs.com
Web: http://www.libertynet.org/flowrsho/village/AIFD.html

For information on certification and course schedules, contact:

American Floral Art School
529 South Wabash Avenue, Suite 610
Chicago, IL 60605
Tel: 312-922-9328

For information on educational opportunities, including online courses, contact:

Rittners School of Floral Design
2345 Marlborough Street
Boston, MA 02115
Tel: 617-267-3824
Web: http://www.tiac.net/users/stevrt/index.html

Franchise Owners

Business **Mathematics**	School Subjects
Following instructions **Leadership/management**	Personal Skills
Primarily one location **Primarily indoors**	Work Environment
High school diploma	Minimum Education Level
$25,000 to $87,000 to $171,000+	Salary Range
None available	Certification or Licensing
Faster than the average	Outlook

Overview

A *franchise owner* contracts with a company to sell the company's products or services. After paying an initial fee, and agreeing to pay the company a certain percentage of revenue, the franchise owner can use the company's name, logo, and guidance. McDonald's, Subway, and Dairy Queen are some of the top franchise opportunities; these companies have franchises all across the country. Franchises account for over 80 billion dollars in annual sales in the United States, and 40 percent of all U.S. retail sales.

History

Know anybody with an antique Singer sewing machine? Chances are, it was originally sold by one of the first franchise operations. During the Civil War the Singer Sewing Machine Company recognized the cost-efficiency of franchising, and allowed dealers across the country to sell its sewing machines. Coca-Cola, as well as the Ford Motor Company and other automobile manufacturers, followed Singer's lead in the early 20th century by granting

own—you've paid a franchise fee, purchased equipment, and rented space. You'll be handling many administrative details, such as record-keeping, creating budgets, and preparing reports for the franchiser. You'll also be hiring employees, scheduling work hours, and preparing payroll. Using the franchiser's marketing methods, you'll advertise your business. The practices and systems of franchisers differ, so you'll need to carefully research the franchise before you buy into it.

You may be working directly with your clientele. Of course, someone who owns multiple units of the McDonald's franchise probably won't be taking orders at the counter; but someone who owns a single unit of a smaller operation, like a pool maintenance service, may be actively involved in the work at hand, and in meeting the customers.

Donna Weber of Redmond, Washington, owns a Jazzercise franchise. Jazzercise is the world's largest dance fitness franchise corporation, with over 4,700 Jazzercise-certified instructors leading workouts for 450,000 students. "I own and teach 7 Jazzercise classes a week, in 2 different suburbs around the Seattle area," Donna says. After investing with an initial low franchise fee, Donna went through much training and testing; the training involves instruction on exercise physiology, dance/exercise technique, and safety issues, as well as instruction on the business aspect of owning a franchise. After training, Donna received certification, and started her business. She pays a monthly fee to Jazzercise, and in return receives choreography notes to new songs, and videos demonstrating the exercises.

In addition to conducting classes, Donna spends some part of every work day preparing paper work for the corporate headquarters. "And I keep track of my students' attendance and write personal postcards to those I haven't seen in a while, those who are having birthdays, those who need some personal recognition for a job well done, etc." Donna must also regularly learn new routines. "I teach three different formats," she says, "regular aerobics, step, and a circuit-training class each week, so there is a lot of prep to do a good, safe class."

Your experience with a franchise will also be affected by the name-recognition of the business. If it's a fairly new business, you may have to take on much of the responsibility of promoting it. If it is a well-established business, customers and clients already know what to expect from your operation.

Requirements

High School

Business, math, economics, and accounting courses will be the most valuable to you in preparing for franchise ownership. Before buying into a franchise, you'll have to do a lot of research into the company, and you'll be analyzing a lot of information, including local demographics, to determine whether a business is a sound investment. English and composition is important for developing communication skills in establishing relationships with franchisers and customers. Join your high school business club to meet local franchisees, and to learn about the issues affecting business owners.

Postsecondary Training

There is certain to be a franchise opportunity for you, no matter what your education background. When franchisers consider your application for the right to purchase a unit, they'll take into consideration your previous experience in the area. Obviously, a real estate company is unlikely to take a risk on you if you've never had any experience as a broker. There are some franchise opportunities that require degrees; for example, to own an environmental consulting agency, a business which helps companies meet government environmental standards, you'll have to be an engineer or geologist. But there are also many companies willing to sell to someone wanting to break into a new business. Franchisers will often include special training as part of the initial franchise fee.

Survey results published by *Franchise Times Magazine* in 1996, showed that 87 percent of franchisees have attended college or have college degrees. This reflects the fact that many franchisees have worked for many years in other professions in order to have the money and security needed for starting new businesses.

Certification or Licensing

You may have to obtain a small business license to own a franchise unit in your state. Because of the varied nature of franchise opportunities, there's no standard certification. Some franchisers, however, have their own certification process and require their franchisees to go through training.

Other Requirements

As with any small business, you need self-motivation and discipline in order to make your franchise unit successful. Though you'll have some help from your franchiser, the responsibilities of ownership are your own. You'll also need a good credit rating to be eligible for a bank loan, or you'll need enough money of your own for the initial investment. You should be a fairly cautious person—many people are taken every year in fraudulent franchise schemes. But at the same time, you should feel comfortable taking some risks.

Exploring

The International Franchise Association (IFA) hosts a very informative Web site, and publishes *Franchising World Magazine*; check out these sources for some insight into the concerns of franchisees. Also, read some of the many business magazines that report on small business opportunities. Many of these magazines, such as *Entrepreneur,* publish special editions dealing specifically with franchises.

Many of the establishments where high school students find part-time jobs are franchise units. If working for McDonald's, Subway, Dairy Queen, or one of the many other franchised restaurants, arrange to meet the owner to discuss the pros and cons of franchise ownership. Or you may want to choose the type of franchise that interests you, then go speak to a local unit owner. Also, most franchise companies will send you brochures about their franchise opportunities.

Employers

There are a number of franchise directories available that list hundreds of franchise opportunities in diverse areas. While some franchisers sell units all across the country, others only do business in a few states. Some of the most successful franchises can guarantee a franchisee great revenue, but these franchise units can require hundreds of thousands of dollars for initial investment.

Many franchisees own more than one franchise unit with a company; some even tie two different franchises together in a practice called "cross-branding." For example, you may own a pizza franchise, as well as an ice cream franchise housed in the same restaurant. Or you may own a convenience store with a fast-food outlet.

Starting Out

Before you invest a cent, or sign any papers, you should do an extensive amount of research into the franchise, particularly if it's a fairly new company. There are many disreputable franchise operations, so you need to be certain of what you're investing in. Lawyers and franchise consultants offer their services to assist people in choosing franchises; some consultants also conduct seminars. The Federal Trade Commission (FTC) publishes *The FTC Consumer Guide to Buying a Franchise* and other relevant publications. IFA also provides franchise-buying advice.

You'll need money for the initial franchise fee and for the expenses of the first few years of business. You may pursue a loan from the bank, from business associates, the Small Business Administration, or you may use your own savings. In some cases your start-up costs will be very low; in others you'll need money for a computer, rental of work space, equipment, signs, and staff. The average start-up cost for a franchise unit is $140,000, but that average includes hotels and motels. A more common cost is between $50,000 and $60,000. Some franchises can cost much less. Donna's Jazzercise franchise required an initial $600 franchise fee. Though her business has been successful, she must share her gross income. "Twenty percent of that goes back to Jazzercise each month as a fee, I pay about 23 percent of the gross for monthly rent, and 8.6 percent to the state of Washington for sales tax collected on the price of my tickets. There are lots of women grossing $75,000 a year doing this, and there are some who choose to do this for fun and make nothing in return. It's all in how you make it work for you."

Advancement

A new franchise unit usually takes a few years to turn profitable. Once your business has proven a success, you may choose to invest in other franchise units with the same company. You may also be able to afford to hire management and other staff to take on some of the many responsibilities of the business.

Earnings

Franchisers will often provide potential franchisees with information about earnings; when making these earnings claims, a franchiser is required to provide proof of them. Gallup poll results published in 1992 stated the average pretax income of franchise owners was $124,290. This figure proved to be controversial—some experts considered the figure too high. But a survey conducted by *Franchise Times Magazine* in 1997 supported the earlier findings. The survey found the median net pretax earnings to be $171,000 a year (including the salaries drawn by the franchisees). The median gross revenue figure was $447,000. Over 27 percent of the survey respondents had gross annual revenues exceeding one million dollars.

Work Environment

Owning your own franchise unit can be demanding, requiring work of 60 to 70 hours a week, but you'll have the satisfaction of knowing that the business's success is a result of your own hard work. You can buy into opportunities that are less demanding, and may only require a part-time commitment. "I'm not getting rich," Donna says, "but I love my job and I love being my own boss. I can schedule my vacations when I want; we usually don't close our classes down, we hire certified Jazzercise substitutes."

The work may be very stressful if you're handling all the details of the business yourself, and dealing with the hiring and management of a staff can also be difficult. In some situations, much of your work will be limited to an office setting; in other situations, such as with a home inspection service or a maid service, you'll be driving to remote sites to work with clients. Some franchises are mobile in nature, and will involve a lot of traveling within a designated region.

Outlook

Entrepreneur Magazine makes predictions about the best franchise opportunities every year; recent trends include juice bars, senior day care, vitamin sales, and a resurgence of frozen yogurt and fitness establishments. Home-based franchises, such as Internet consulting, mystery shopping, and career coaching, are expected to increase in popularity. The success of an individual franchise unit will depend on the fads of the time, the popularity of the product or service, and the number of franchise units in your region.

While some experts say that the success rate of franchises is very high, and a great deal of money can be made with a franchise unit, others say franchising isn't as successful as starting an independent business. According to the Department of Commerce, less than 5 percent of franchised outlets have failed each year since 1971. However, when reporting figures, franchisers don't always consider a unit as failing if it is under different ownership, but still in operation.

For More Information

For general information about franchising, and to learn about specific franchise opportunities, contact:

International Franchise Association (IFA)
1350 New York Avenue, NW, Suite 900
Washington, DC 20005-4709
Tel: 202-628-8000
Email: ifa@franchise.org
Web: http://www.franchise.org

For FTC publications regarding franchising, contact:

Public Reference Branch
Federal Trade Commission
Washington, DC 20580
Tel: 202-326-3128
Web: http://www.ftc.gov

For other information about buying a franchise, contact:

American Association of Franchisees and Dealers
PO Box 81887
San Diego, CA 92138-1887
Tel: 800-733-9858
Web: http://www.aafd.org

Greeting Card Designers and Writers

Art English Computer science	School Subjects
Artistic Communication/ideas	Personal Skills
Primarily indoors Primarily one location	Work Environment
High school diploma	Minimum Education Level
$15/idea to $50/idea to $150/idea	Salary Range
None available	Certification or Licensing
About as fast as the average	Outlook

Overview

Greeting card designers and writers either work freelance or as staff members of greeting card and gift manufacturers. Designers use artistic skills to create illustrated or photographic images for cards, posters, mugs, and other items generally sold in card shops; writers compose the expressions, poems, and jokes that accompany the images. The Greeting Card Association estimates that there are more than 1,500 large and small greeting card publishers in America.

History

The Valentine is considered by many to be the earliest form of greeting card. Up until the fifth century, Romans celebrated a fertility festival called Lupercalia every February 15. At the feast, women wrote love notes and dropped them in an urn; the men would pick a note from the urn, then seek the company of the woman who composed the note. But the mass-produced holiday cards we know today didn't really originate until the 1880s in England and America. With printing costs and postage rates low, the colorful, cheerful, and beautifully illustrated cards of the day quickly grew in popularity.

The Job

From statements of love to rude insults, the contemporary greeting card industry provides a note for practically every expression. Hallmark and American Greetings are the biggest names in the business, offering cards for many occasions; other card companies have carved out their own individual niches, like C-ya ("relationship closure cards" to send to ex-boyfriends, former bosses, and anybody you don't ever want to see again) and Mixed Blessing (which sells "interfaith and multicultural holiday products" such as cards and products that combine symbols of Christmas and Hanukkah, including the book "Blintzes for Blitzen"). Though some of these companies use the talents of full-time staff writers and designers, others rely on freelancers to submit ideas, images, and expressions. In addition to greeting card production, some companies buy words and images for email greetings, and for lines of products like mugs, posters, pillows, and balloons.

Bonnie Neubauer, a freelance writer in Pennsylvania, has tapped into the "business to business" greeting card niche. "They're tools to help sales people," Bonnie explains. "They help business people keep in touch." She sells her ideas to a small company called IntroKnocks, but many greeting card companies are getting into the business of business-to-business cards. Hallmark and Gibson, two of the biggest card manufacturers, now sell cards to brighten up the workplace. "So many people communicate through faxes, emails, voicemail," Bonnie says, "that when a card comes in a colored envelope, with a hand-written address, it gets attention." To spark ideas, Bonnie reads industry trade magazines, visits company Web sites, and looks over a book of stock photos. Once recognizing a business need, she comes up with a card to meet the need. "Some people only send out cartoons," she says about the business-to-business greeting card marketplace, "some people are more serious, and want only cards with sophisticated photographs."

Working from home offices, greeting card writers and designers come up with their ideas, then submit them to the companies for consideration. "Coming up with good card ideas," Bonnie says, "involves taking cliches, and combining them with a tad of humor." Artists and photographers submit reproductions of their work, rather than their originals, because some companies don't return unaccepted submissions or may lose the submissions in the review process. Artists submit prints, color xeroxes, duplicate transparencies, or floppy disks. Writers submit their ideas on index cards (one idea per index card).

Requirements

High School

Hone your writing and artistic skills in high school by taking English and art classes. Since many designers use computers to create their designs, computer science courses also will be helpful.

Postsecondary Training

College education is not necessary for freelancing as an artist and writer, though card companies looking to hire you for a full-time staff position may require a background in English, creative writing, graphic design, or commercial arts. Even if you only want to freelance, community college courses that instruct you in the use of computer design programs can help you to create professional-looking images for submission to companies.

Certification or Licensing

No certification program exists for greeting card writers/designers. But if you decide to print your own cards and sell them to stores and representatives, you may be required by your state to maintain a business license.

Other Requirements

"I'm extremely self-motivated," Bonnie says, in regard to making her home business a success, "and grossly optimistic." As for the writing itself, Bonnie emphasizes the importance of a sense of humor. "I love word-play," she says, "and I love marketing and promotions." Any writer and designer should also be patient, persistent, and capable of taking rejection.

Exploring

Try writing and designing your own greeting cards. There are many software programs that will help you create attractive cards, stationery, and newsletters. Ask your high school English teacher or counselor to set up an interview with a greeting card designer or freelance writer.

Employers

As a freelancer, you can work anywhere in the country, and submit your work through the mail. *Writer's Market*, a reference book published annually by Writer's Digest Books, includes a section listing the greeting card companies that accept submissions from freelance writers and artists. While some companies only buy a few ideas a year, others buy hundreds of ideas. Hallmark, by far the largest greeting card manufacturer, doesn't accept unsolicited ideas, but hires many creative people for full-time staff positions. Because of Hallmark's reputation as a great employer, competition for those positions is high.

Starting Out

Get to know the market by visiting local card shops; find out what's popular, and what kinds of cards each company sells. Visit the Web sites of the greeting card companies listed in *Writer's Market* and study their online catalogs. Most companies have very specific guidelines—one may publish only humorous cards, while another may only publish inspirational poems. Once you have a good sense of what companies might be interested in your work, write them or call them to find out their submission guidelines. Also, each spring, Hallmark holds an annual competition for their writing and editing internships.

Advancement

After you've submitted a lot of your work to many different companies, you'll begin to make connections with people in the business. These connections can be valuable, and may result in better pay (such as royalties and percentages) and exclusive contracts. As you get to know the business better, you may choose to produce and market your own line of cards. Sally Silagy, who owns Gardening Greetings, sells a Home-Based Greeting Card Kit, which details her own experiences with starting a business, and offers instruction into how to get started.

Earnings

Salaries vary widely among freelance greeting card writers/designers. Designers and artists can typically make more money for their work than writers. Some card designer/writers sell only a few ideas a year. Others make a great deal of money, working exclusively with a company, or by manufacturing and distributing their own lines of cards and products. Card companies typically pay freelancers fees for each idea they buy. Some companies may offer a royalty payment plan, including an initial advance. A small company may pay as little as $15 for an idea, while a larger company may pay $150 or more.

Work Environment

Both as a writer and as a designer, you'll be spending much of your time in your home office. Some of your time will be in front of the computer, designing images, or writing copy. Coming up with the initial ideas, however, may involve pampering yourself so that you can be at your most creative—many artists have certain routines to inspire them, such as listening to music, looking at photography and art books, or reading a novel.

Outlook

According to the Greeting Card Association (an organization representing card companies), the greeting card industry's retail sales have increased steadily from $2.1 billion in 1980, to over $7 billion in 1997. From designing animated email messages to greeting card CD-ROM programs, greeting card writers/designers will likely find more and more outlets for their work. Advances in Web technology should also aid the card designer who can post ideas and images, and invite companies to browse, download, and pay for the ideas on-line.

For More Information

For an application for Hallmark's internship program, write to:

Hallmark-CRWEB
Creative Writing Summer Intern Competition
Creative Staffing and Development, #444
2501 McGee
Kansas City, MO 64108
Web: http://www.hallmark.com

For price and other information for Sally Silagy's Home-Based Greeting Card Kit, which details how to start your own greeting card business, contact:

Gardening Greetings
189a Paradise Circle
Woodland Park, CO 80863
Web: http://www.gardeninggreetings.com

Lawn/Gardening Service Owners

Agriculture Technical/Shop	School Subjects
Following instructions Mechanical/manipulative	Personal Skills
Primarily outdoors Primarily multiple locations	Work Environment
High school diploma	Minimum Education Level
$15,000 to $35,000 to $50,000	Salary Range
Voluntary	Certification or Licensing
About as fast as the average	Outlook

Overview

The owners of lawn and gardening services maintain the lawns of residential and commercial properties. They cut grass and shrubbery, clean yards, and treat grass with fertilizer and insecticide. They may also landscape, which involves the arrangement of lawns, trees, and bushes. There are over a million people employed in some aspect of the lawn care industry. One out of every four landscapers, groundskeepers, and nursery workers are self-employed.

History

Have you ever visited or seen photographs of the Taj Mahal in India, or Versailles in France? Then you've seen some elaborate examples of the lawns and gardens of the world. For as long as people have built grand palaces, they've designed lawns and gardens to surround them. Private, irrigated gardens of ancient Egypt and Persia were regarded as paradise with their thick, green vegetation and cool shade. In the 16th century, Italians kept gardens that wound about fountains, columns, and steps. The English developed the "cottage-style" gardens to adhere to the natural surroundings. Early American gardens, such as those surrounding Monticello in Virginia, were inspired by this English style.

The English also inspired the Georgian style of house design in the 18th century which caught on across Europe and America. Rows of houses down city blocks were designed as units, their yards hidden behind the houses and away from the streets. Lawn care as a business blossomed with the growth of the United States and home ownership between the Civil War and World War I. Golf also became popular among the rich at this time, spurring the development of lawn care products and machinery. After World War II, many people hired lawn maintenance professionals, or the teenager down the street looking for summer work, to cut the grass and trim the shrubs.

The Job

If you've made some extra money mowing lawns for your neighbors, then you're already familiar with many of the aspects of a lawn care service. Walking behind a power mower during the hottest days of the year may make you miserable, but keeping lawns looking nice can be a great opportunity for self-employment. Private homes, apartment complexes, golf courses, and parks are some of the properties that require regular lawn maintenance.

According to a Gallup survey, more than 22 million U.S. households spent $14.6 billion on professional lawn services in 1997. The benefits of a nice lawn aren't just aesthetic; a well-kept lawn can increase property values, provide a safe place for children to play, and improve the environment.

You may choose to offer only a few services, such as lawn mowing and hedge clipping. But some businesses offer a large number of services, from simple cleaning to the actual design of the yard. Some lawn services specialize in organic lawn care. These services don't use harmful chemicals to treat lawns, but rather rely on organic-based fertilizers and biological controls for insects and diseases.

When working for private homeowners, you'll do yard work once or twice a week for each client. With a truck or van, you'll arrive at the residence with your own equipment, which may include a push or riding mower, an aerator, and a blower vac. You'll cut the grass, as well as "weed-eat" (trim the weeds at the edges of the houses and fences). You'll also apply fertilizer and insecticide to the lawn to keep the grass healthy. The lawn's health will also be aided by an aerator, a tool you run over the yard to make holes in the top soil.

You'll also plant grass seed in areas where there is little growth. You'll use the blow vac to blow leaves from the yard, sidewalks, and driveway. Other debris, such as tree branches, dirt, and other materials may litter the yard; you'll pick up this debris and haul it away in your truck. Lawn services are often called in after storms and other natural disasters to repair lawns.

"There are a lot of little services you can throw in to keep you busy," says Sam Morgan, who has operated a lawn care service in Dallas, Texas, for the last four years. He does general lawn maintenance for residential yards, as well as some rental properties. "Having some rental property can be good," he says. "It's year-round work. But it can also be dirty work; you have to pick up a lot of trash." In addition to mowing yards and weed-eating, he'll assist with planting flower beds, cleaning house gutters, and some light tree work.

Tree care involves the pruning and trimming of branches. You may also be asked to remove dead, or unwanted, trees and to plant new ones. You may also offer landscaping services in which you'll be involved in arranging the lawn. You'll assist in positioning trees, bushes, fountains, flower beds, and lighting. You may also put up wood or metal fencing, and install sprinkler systems.

"I started the business on a shoestring," Sam says. "But I learned early that you have to have good equipment." He now owns a commercial mower that can handle 200 yards a week. In addition to the actual yard work, Sam must attend to business details, such as keeping tax records, making phone calls, and preparing estimates and bills.

Requirements

High School

Take agriculture, voc-tech, and other courses that will help you get familiar with the machinery, fertilizers, and chemicals used in lawn maintenance. Agriculture courses will also teach you about different grasses and plants, and how to care for them. Join organizations such as Future Farmers of

America and 4-H to gain experience with horticulture. Business and accounting courses will teach you about record-keeping, budgeting, and finances.

Postsecondary Training

You don't really need a college education to start your own lawn care service, though a community college course in small business management could be beneficial. You can learn about lawn maintenance on the job, either by assisting someone with an established lawn care business, or by taking on a few residential customers. The Professional Lawn Care Association of America (PLCAA) has a national technician training program. Some franchisers also include management training with the initial franchise fee.

Certification or Licensing

Some states require licensing of lawn care professionals who use pest control products. Certification isn't required, but PLCAA sponsors the "Principles of Turfgrass Management" course. Though the course is offered through the University of Georgia, it is available nationally on a home-study basis. Graduates of the course earn the title Certified Turfgrass Professional.

Other Requirements

You'll be promoting your business yourself, and relying on good word of mouth, so you'll need to have people skills. "I'm a good salesman," Sam says. He also emphasizes that he's committed to doing a quality job for every customer. You should have an eye for detail, so that you'll be sure to notice all the areas where the lawn needs work. You should also be in fairly good health to withstand working in the heat of the summer. You'll also need to be self-motivated in order to seek out more customers and build your business.

Exploring

Opportunities to learn how to care for a lawn and garden are no further than your own backyard. If you have access to a lawn, experiment with planting and gardening. There are a number of magazines and books that include articles on lawn and garden care, and cable television stations, such as Home and Garden TV (HGTV), feature programming about gardening. Also, look into volunteer and part-time work with botanical gardens, greenhouses, and park and recreation crews.

Every summer, many high school students find reliable work mowing lawns. But many of these students tire of the work early in the summer. Be persistent in seeking out work all summer long. You should also be committed to doing good work; you'll have stiff competition from professional lawn care businesses that offer more services, have commercial machinery, and have knowledge of fertilizers and pesticides. Some lawn care companies also hire students for summer work.

Employers

Most of your clients will be private homeowners, though you may contract with commercial properties. Condos, hotels, apartment complexes, golf courses, sports fields, and parks all require regular lawn service.

There are a number of franchise opportunities in lawn care that, for a fee, will assist you in promoting your business and building a clientele. Emerald Green Lawn Care, Liqui-Green Lawn Care, and Lawn Doctor are just a few. NaturaLawn of America is a franchise of organic-based lawn care.

Starting Out

Sam's lawn service isn't his first venture into entrepreneurship; he's also owned a number of dry cleaners. After selling the dry cleaners, he went to work for a chemical company. When the company downsized, Sam was faced with finding a new job. "I just went to Sears and bought a mower," he says. Since then, he's been able to invest in commercial machinery that can better handle the demands of the work, and he's found a number of ways to increase business. "I bill once a month," he says. "I get more business that way." He's also expanding his service to include some light landscaping, such as shrub work and planting small trees.

Depending on how you approach your business, your start-up costs can be quite low. To purchase commercial quality equipment, your initial investment will be between $3,000 and $4,000. A franchise, however, will cost thousands of dollars more. For around $50,000, you should be able to invest in a franchise opportunity; this investment will include the initial fee, equipment, computer, inventory, and van down payment.

Advancement

When you've established your business, you can expand your services. Some lawn professionals offer equipment and supply sales. You may also be able to get large contracts with golf courses and sports fields. With some additional schooling, you can pursue work as a landscape architect. Sam currently has one employee, but he hopes for his business to grow more, allowing him to hire others. "I don't want to be doing so much of the physical work," he says.

Earnings

The money you'll make from your lawn care service will depend on a number of factors—your geographic location, the size of your business, and your years as a lawn care professional. Obviously, a lawn care service will make more money in an area of the country that has mild winters and more months of lawn growth. Also, a lawn care professional with a small clientele may make less than $20,000 a year, while a franchise lawn care company with a number of contracts and a large staff can make hundreds of thousands. A salary survey, published by *Grounds Maintenance* magazine in 1997, found that grounds managers make an average of $37,410 a year.

Work Environment

You may find mowing lawns and trimming shrubs relaxing, and you may enjoy having the opportunity to work outdoors during the pleasant days of spring and summer. But the work can also be exhausting and strenuous. You'll be lifting equipment from your truck, and you'll be doing a lot of walking, kneeling, and bending. You may also be climbing trees. Depending on the nature of your business, you may be handling chemicals. And the machinery you use (lawn mowers, weed eaters, blow vacs) will be noisy.

"Most likely," Sam says, "during the spring and summer, you can make plenty of money. There's plenty of work to be done." But some of that work may be in the hottest days of the summer, or on rainy days. With your own service, you can arrange to work regular weekday hours, or you can schedule weekends.

Outlook

A good future is predicted for lawn care services. A Gallup survey found a recent annual increase of $600 million in lawn care spending. The sale of lawn care products is expected to reach over $4 billion a year. It is anticipated that this increased spending will continue as more houses are built and more people recognize the importance of quality lawn care. The Environmental Protection Agency is publicizing the environmental benefits of a healthy lawn, emphasizing that healthy grass controls dust and pollens, provides oxygen, and improves the quality of groundwater. More people are also recognizing that a nice lawn can increase home value, as much as 15 percent according to studies. Technology will also aid the industry. With better, more economical equipment, lawn care professionals can do more specialized work in less time, allowing them to keep their service fees low.

For More Information

To learn about certification, training, and facts about the lawn care industry, contact:

Professional Lawn Care Association of America (PLCAA)
1000 Johnson Ferry Road, NE, Suite C-135
Marietta, GA 30068
Tel: 770-977-5222
Web: http://www.plcaa.org

Medical Billing Service Owners

School Subjects
- Computer science
- Mathematics

Personal Skills
- Following instructions
- Leadership/management

Work Environment
- Primarily one location
- Primarily indoors

Minimum Education Level
- Some postsecondary training

Salary Range
- $10,000 to $50,000 to $75,000

Certification or Licensing
- Voluntary

Outlook
- About as fast as the average

Overview

Medical billers help doctors and other health care professionals get payment for services. They send bills to patients, private insurance companies, Medicare, and other insurers. Using special software, they file insurance claims electronically via a computer modem. They keep files on patients and insurers, and use medical codes when filing claims. Most billers work from their home offices, though some work in the offices of doctors and clinics. Medical billers are sometimes known as *electronic billing professionals, claims processing professionals,* and *medical provider consultants.*

History

Group health insurance plans first developed in the 1940s as a result of the growing expense of medical care. Since then, doctors have received much of their payment from insurance companies, rather than individual patients. With more patients using these "third-party" payers, doctors began to need assistance in dealing with the extra work of completing and submitting insurance forms. Medical billing services developed in response to this demand. Accountants, administrative assistants, and people working at home took on the bookkeeping responsibilities of doctors' offices. When personal computers came into common use in the 1980s, medical billing changed from paper-based claims to electronic claims. Filing claims electronically required modems and specially designed software, and medical billing services were in even greater demand; doctors didn't have the time to learn the complexities of submitting electronic claims. Demand for outside billing services increased even more after 1990, when the federal government ruled that doctors, and not elderly patients, were responsible for submitting claims to Medicare.

The Job

No matter how many injuries or illnesses you may have had in high school, you probably have not had much experience with insurance companies. Your parents, however, have certainly dealt with the responsibilities of maintaining insurance coverage for the family. They've saved bills, submitted claims, and dealt with doctors' offices and insurance agencies. Health care coverage is considered an important and necessary benefit of full-time employment, so much so that many people make job decisions based on the quality of insurance available. Insurance has become a major concern as people struggle to meet the rising costs of health care.

So you can imagine the difficulties facing doctors in billing patients, filing claims, and keeping accurate patient accounts. In addition to private insurance companies, doctors receive payment from Medicare (a government insurance program for people over the age of 65, and for people with disabilities), Medicaid (a government insurance program for people of all ages within certain income limits), and worker's compensation (insurance from employers to cover employees injured on the job). In order to get paid by these insurers, doctors must submit detailed claims. These claims include information about diagnosis and treatment, and require a knowledge of medical codes.

As a medical biller, you'll handle the filing of these claims. You'll work out of your home, and take on as many clients as you choose. According to Merl Coslick, the director of the Electronic Medical Billing Network of America, Inc., a national trade association, the majority of medical billers have three or fewer clients. Medical billing is often seen as supplementary income, and more than three clients may require a staff and much more time. Felicitas Cortez is one of these billers keeping her service small to allow her to work from her home office and spend time with her children. Her father is a physician, and part of his practice involves managing a nursing home. Felicitas handles the billing for the nursing home patients. Most of the patients are on Medicare. Felicitas designed a form which the doctor takes with him when visiting patients. For each patient's form, the doctor lists what services the patient requires, along with his diagnosis. Once a month, these forms are sent to Felicitas, who maintains records for the patients. "The record includes insurance information, such as the Medicare number, if the patient is on public aid, and if there's any secondary insurance," Felicitas says.

Felicitas must also convert the doctor's diagnosis to a special medical code. Medical billers use ICD codes which represent diagnoses, and CPT codes which represent treatment procedures. These codes are standard for private insurers across the country, and for Medicare. "I have a book to consult for the codes," Felicitas says, "but it can get complicated. I don't have a medical background, and there are so many kinds of pneumonia, for example. There are about 100 codes for pneumonia, and insurers are very particular." Once she has the codes she needs, Felicitas can file a claim. Though a few insurers still accept claims submitted on paper, most require electronic filing. Electronic claims have proven cheaper than paper billing, and they speed up processing by several weeks. Felicitas uses a software system called Medical Office Management Systems (MOMS), designed specifically for medical billing. After getting online, Felicitas lists the place of service, the ICD code, the CPT code, and the cost of the visit, and electronically submits this claim to a clearinghouse. A clearinghouse is a service that routes the claims to both the primary and secondary insurers. She does this once a week, and reconciles accounts once a month. Payment goes directly from the insurer to the doctor, so Felicitas must check with the doctor's office to keep track of paid claims.

But your work doesn't just involve computers. You'll be making many phone calls to insurers and doctors to ensure that claims are paid. Felicitas must also speak to family members of the nursing home patients to determine how deductibles are to be met.

Though some medical billers handle only insurance claims, others offer many services. Your medical billing service may also send bills to individual patients. You may deal with insurance companies for your clients, following up on claims. You'll also have to maintain your own financial records, such as business expenses for tax purposes, and payment received from doctors.

Requirements

High School

You'll be using computers, online services, and special software as a medical biller, so take classes in computer fundamentals and computer programming. Communication and English courses will help you develop the phone skills needed. With accounting, math, and business management classes, you'll learn how to keep accurate financial records. Though a medical background isn't necessary, some familiarity with health issues and the health care industry will help you to understand insurance, doctors' offices, and treatments. Take a course in health to gain this familiarity. A business club will allow you to meet local small business owners, and teach you about some of the demands of home-based business ownership.

Postsecondary Training

Medical billers come from a variety of different educational and professional backgrounds. A college education will assist you in soliciting clients, and in performing the billing duties, but it isn't required. Some background in medicine and health care can be helpful to you, but a degree in business management, or in English, can be equally beneficial. You can also benefit from office experience, and an understanding of administrative procedures. Some community colleges offer medical claims billing classes; conferences and workshops in medical billing are also offered by Medicare, private insurers, and clearinghouses.

The billing software you choose for your business may include special training. Two professional associations offer instruction: The National Association of Claims Processing Professionals (NACPP) and The Electronic

Medical Billing Network of America (EMBN). The NACPP holds seminars and training classes for its members. These seminars deal with the topics of medical terminology, office management, insurance forms, and billing software. The EMBN offers training courses in the New Jersey area, and also distributes computer-based training packages nationwide. Courses include instruction in setting up a medical billing service, billing center management procedures, and claim billing procedures.

Certification or Licensing

Certification isn't required, but it is available from both the EMBN and the NACPP upon completion of their training courses. After completing the EMBN training course, you'll take the Certified Electronic Medical Biller (CEMB) exam to test your understanding of the business. Other associations, clearinghouses, and software companies also offer certification training courses. Many medical billing professionals work without any kind of certification or licensing at all, but certification can help you in promoting your business to clients.

Other Requirements

You'll need the patience required for filling out long, detailed forms, transforming treatments and diagnoses to codes, and maintaining client records. You should be organized, and have an understanding of spreadsheet programs, word processing programs, and online services. Obviously, a head for figures is important, but people skills are also very valuable. Felicitas must deal sensitively with the nursing care patients and their families in discussing payments and insurance deductibles, but must be firm and persistent when dealing with insurance companies. "You'll have to speak to a lot of different people in different ways to get what you need," she says. You'll also have to keep up on laws affecting insurers, doctors, and billing methods.

Exploring

There are many volunteer opportunities in the health care industry available to high school students. Assisting at a hospital or nursing home will give you some background in medical terminology and a doctor's routine. Working part-time for a pharmacist can give you similar experience, and may include working with Medicare and Medicaid forms, and preparing medications for nursing homes. Many school clubs elect treasurers who handle receipts, payments, and bills; either volunteer for the position, or assist the adviser in charge of money matters. A part-time administrative position with a local insurance agency, or any area business, can give you valuable experience in handling calls, preparing forms, and billing procedures.

Employers

From chiropractors to psychiatrists, health care professionals must deal with insurers, billing patients, and keeping accurate payment records. Anybody needing to file claims with third-party payers, including personal trainers and physical therapists, can benefit from the services of a medical billing professional. You may work with one specific area of health care, or you may have a diverse clientele. Your clients may be in your local area, or you may work with clients in other cities, contacting them by phone, fax, and email.

Starting Out

You should try to get some experience with medical billing before investing in the business. Working in a doctor's office can quickly familiarize you with the job's requirements, and will give you experience that you can promote to potential clients. You'll want to be very sure that the business is for you, because start-up costs can run into thousands of dollars. You'll need a computer and printer, database and marketing software, and medical billing software. Be very careful about what billing software you select; there are many different programs available, and some cost upwards of $10,000. Many programs cost much less, however, and may offer all you need for a small business. The price of a software program may also include additional services, such as access to a clearinghouse that routes your electronic claims to primary and secondary insurers.

You'll also want to make sure you can take on enough clients to support your business. Most general care physicians have their own billing staffs. You'll have to convince these doctors that they'll benefit from bringing in an outside billing service, and that you have the skills to handle the billing and improve payment methods. By joining a professional association, you can receive guidance and support from other medical billers. Ted Miller of the NACPP says his organization serves as an information source—members regularly receive emails directing them to relevant Web sites, and they also have access to an online forum of messages, questions, and support.

Advancement

The majority of people with their own billing services prefer to keep their businesses small, handling only a few clients. But it is possible to expand your business into a service for several doctors. According to Merl Coslick of the EMBN, there are about 600 companies grossing over a million dollars a year and processing tens of thousands of claims a week. Obviously, you'll need to invest much more money into growing a large company—you'll need a staff, additional office equipment, and commercial office space.

But you can still advance into other areas while maintaining a small operation. Some experienced billing professionals serve as consultants for doctors' offices. They train an office's internal billing staff, help build billing records, and oversee the electronic claims filing.

Earnings

Some medical billers charge their clients for each claim processed; others charge a percentage of the insurance payment. Some billers have contracts with doctors and charge flat weekly or monthly fees. No salary surveys have yet been conducted on independent billing service owners, but Coslick estimates that a service processing 300 claims per month can make $10,000 per year for each client. Though most owners of medical billing services choose to operate only part-time, those working full-time may be able to process 1,500 claims or more per month.

Work Environment

Most of your work will be done in the comfort of your own home office. Though you won't have any supervision, you will have clients regularly contacting you to check on the status of an insurance payment. You'll spend much of your time on the phone, and on the computer. In some cases, you may visit a client's office to collect forms; some billers, however, simply use fax machines and messenger services to exchange information. If you also offer consulting services, you'll be spending some of your time in doctors' offices working closely with billing staff members. Your hours per week will depend on your number of clients. Serving only a few clients will require approximately 20 hours a week; any more than 3 clients, and you'll be putting in 40 hours or more. Because much of your work is done at the computer using electronic systems, you don't always have to work regular business hours. You can set your own schedule, working evenings and weekends if you prefer.

Outlook

Though many Americans are still without health insurance, some government programs are actively involved in providing insurance to the elderly, children, people with disabilities, and those with low incomes. The Health Care Financing Administration (HCFA), which administers Medicare, Medicaid, and Child Health Insurance, provides health insurance for over 75 million Americans. This number will increase as the baby boomer generation grows older, and as the newly formed Child Health program evolves. An HCFA study projected health care expenditures to exceed $2 trillion by 2007. This will mean the filing of billions of insurance claims. Doctors will require even more assistance in billing, and receiving payments, particularly as more billing procedures are done electronically. Merl Coslick believes that more billing professionals will become consultants to doctors' offices. Within 3 to 5 years, he predicts, the bulk of billing will be done internally, and consultants will be needed to train staff in medical billing software.

For More Information

Visit the EMBN Web site to learn more about the career of medical biller, subscribe to a monthly newsletter, and to learn about training and publications.

Electronic Medical Billing Network of America, Inc.
PO Box 7162
Watchung, NJ 07060
Tel: 908-757-1211
Email: embn@webcircle.com
Web: http://webcircle.com/embn/index.html

For information about training, medical billing software, and association membership, contact:

National Association of Claims Processing Professionals
1940 East Thunderbird Road, Suite 100
Phoenix, AZ 85022-5787
Tel: 602-867-9377
Email: nacpp@efamedical.com
Web: http://www.nacpp.org

For information about government insurance programs and health care statistics, contact:

Health Care Financing Administration (HCFA)
7500 Security Boulevard
Baltimore, MD 21244
Tel: 410-786-3000
Web: http://www.hcfa.gov

Online Researchers

Computer science English Journalism	School Subjects
Communication/ideas Technical/scientific	Personal Skills
Primarily one location Primarily indoors	Work Environment
Bachelor's degree	Minimum Education Level
$12,000 to $48,000 to $90,000+	Salary Range
Voluntary	Certification or Licensing
About as fast as the average	Outlook

Overview

Online researchers, sometimes called *information brokers* or *independent information professionals,* compile information from online databases and services. They work for clients in a number of different professions, researching marketing surveys, newspaper articles, business and government statistics, abstracts, and other sources of information. They prepare reports and presentations based on their research. There are around 2,000 information brokers in the United States. Online researchers have home-based operations, or they work full-time for libraries, law offices, government agencies, and corporations.

History

Strange as it may seem, some of the earliest examples of online researchers are the keepers of a library established by Ptolemy I (367?-283? BC) in Egypt in the 3rd century BC. These librarians helped to build the first great library by copying and revising classical Greek texts. The monks of Europe also performed some of the modern-day researcher's tasks by building libraries and printing books. Despite their great efforts, libraries weren't used extensively until the 18th century, when literacy increased among the general population. In 1803, the first public library in the United States opened in Connecticut.

In the late 1800s and early 1900s, many different kinds of library associations evolved, reflecting the number of special libraries already established (such as medical and law libraries). With all the developments of the 20th century, these library associations helped to promote special systems and tools for locating information. These systems eventually developed into the online databases and Internet search engines used today. The Internet, although created in 1969 and subsidized by the government as a communication system for the Department of Defense, didn't become a significant source of information until relaxed government policies allowed for its commercial use in 1991.

The Job

Think your many bleary-eyed hours surfing the Net and hanging out in chat rooms have qualified you for work as an online researcher? Well, probably not. Although your interest in the Internet and your computer skills are important to success as an independent information broker, you'll need to understand much more than just search engines. In addition to such Internet services as Alta Vista and Infoseek, you'll need to master Dialog, Lexis/Nexis, and other information databases. You'll also have to compile information with those creaky, old-fashioned devices—fax machines, photocopiers, and telephones. And some situations will require footwork. If this sounds like the work of a private eye, you're not far off; as a matter of fact, some information brokers have worked as private investigators. Private eyes also hire the services of online researchers to assist in their investigations.

A majority of research projects, however, are marketing-based. Suppose a company wants to embark on a new, risky venture: maybe a fruit distribution company wants to make figs as popular as apples and oranges. First, they might want to know some basic information about fig consumption. How many people have even eaten a fig? What articles about figs have been published in national magazines? What have been recent annual sales of figs, Fig Newtons, and other fig-based treats? What popular recipes include figs? For all this information, the company will hire consultants, marketing experts, and researchers. Although individual researchers have their own varied approaches to accomplishing tasks, every researcher must first get to know the subject. A researcher may specialize in a particular area; perhaps you've already worked with retail and distribution, and are very familiar with the trade associations, publications, and other sources of industry information. If not, you'll need to learn as much as you can, as quickly as you can, about the lingo and language of the fruit distribution industry. This means taking some time surfing the Internet, using basic search engines to get a sense of what kind of information is available. The researcher will then move onto a database service, such as the popular Dialog system. These databases provide much more information than the Internet. They make available billions of pages of text and images, including complete newspaper and magazine articles, wire service stories, and company profiles. But using database services can cost a lot of money if you're not familiar with them. Because database services charge the user for the time spent searching, or documents viewed, online researchers must know all the various tips and commands for efficient searching. Once the search is complete, and you've downloaded the information needed, you must prepare the information for the company. You may be expected to make a presentation to the company or to write a complete report. You'll need to know how to use your word processing and graphics programs in order to create the pie graphs, charts, and other illustrations to accompany the text.

"This isn't the kind of profession you can do right out of high school or college," says Mary Ellen Bates, an independent information professional based in Washington, DC. "It requires expertise in searching the professional online services. You can't learn them on your own time; you have to have real-world experience as an online researcher. Many of the most successful information brokers are former librarians." Her success in the business has led her to serve as president of the Association of Independent Information Professionals (AIIP), to write and publish articles about the business, and to serve as a consultant to libraries and other organizations. Recently, she's been hired to research the market for independent living facilities for senior citizens, and the impact of large grocery chains on independent grocery stores. She's also been asked to find some funny stories about the Year 2000 problem, and to find out what rental car companies do with cars after they're past their prime. "Keep in mind that you need a lot more than Internet research skills," Bates says. "You need the ability to run a business from the top to bottom. That means accounting, marketing, collections, strategic planning, and personnel management."

The expense of the commercial database services has affected the career of another online researcher, Sue Carver of Richland, Washington. Changes in Dialog's usage rates have required her to seek out other ways to use her library skills. In addition to such services as market research and document delivery, Carver's Web page promotes a book-finding service, helping people to locate collectible and out-of-print books. "I have found this a fun, if not highly lucrative, activity which puts me in contact with a wide variety of people," she says. "This is a case where the Internet opens the door to other possibilities. Much of this business is repackaging information to a form people want to buy. This is limited only by your imagination." But she also emphasizes that the job of online researcher requires highly specialized skills in information retrieval. "Non-librarians often do not appreciate the vast array of reference material that existed before the Internet," she says, "nor how much librarians have contributed to the information age." Carver holds an MA in library science and has worked as a reference librarian, which involved her with searches on patents, molecular biology, and other technical subjects. She has also worked as an indexer on a nuclear engineering project, and helped plan a search and retrieval system on a separate nuclear project.

Requirements

High School

You'll need to take computer classes to learn how to use word processing and illustration programs and how to use Internet search engines. Any class offered by your high school or public library on information retrieval will familiarize you with database searches and such services as Dialog, Lexis/Nexis, and Dow Jones. English and composition courses are very important, as you'll be expected to write clearly. You'll also be expected to speak in front of clients during presentations, so take a speech and theater class. Journalism classes, and working on your high school newspaper, will involve you directly in information retrieval and writing.

Postsecondary Training

You should start with a good liberal arts program in a college or university, then pursue a master's degree in either a subject specialty or in library and information science. By studying a specific area, such as chemistry or engineering, you can learn the subject from the inside, then offer your expertise to clients looking for knowledgeable research and reports in that area.

Many online researchers have master's degrees in library science. The American Library Association (ALA) accredits library and information science programs and offers a number of scholarships. Courses in library programs deal with techniques of data collection and analysis, use of graphical presentation of sound and text, and networking and telecommunications. Internships are also available in some library science programs.

Continuing education courses are important for online researchers with advanced degrees. Because of the rapidly changing technology, researchers need to attend seminars and take courses and seminars through such organizations as the Special Libraries Association (SLA), and the Information Professionals Institute (IPI). The IPI seminars, conducted in major cities across the country, deal with starting a business, finding clients, online searching, and other topics relevant to both the experienced and the inexperienced information brokers. Many online researchers take additional courses in their subject matter specialization. Mary Ellen attends meetings of the Society for Competitive Intelligence Professionals, since a lot of her work is in the field of competitive intelligence.

Other Requirements

In addition to all the varied computer skills necessary to success as an online researcher, you must have good communication skills. "You're marketing all the time," Mary Ellen says. "If you're not comfortable marketing yourself and speaking publicly, you'll never make it in this business." To keep your business running, you need persistence to pursue new clients and sources of information. You'll be your own boss, so you'll have to be self-motivated in order to meet deadlines. Good record-keeping skills will help you manage the financial, tax, and billing details of the business and help you keep track of important contacts.

Carver advises that you keep up on current events, and that you pay close attention to detail. You should welcome the challenge of locating hard-to-find facts and articles. "I have a logical mind," Carver says, " and love puzzles and mysteries."

Exploring

If you've ever had to write an extensive research paper, then you've probably already had experience with online research. In college, many of your term papers will require that you become familiar with Lexis/Nexis and other library systems. The reference librarians of your school and public libraries should be happy to introduce you to the various library tools available. On the Internet, experiment with the search engines; each service has slightly different features and capabilities.

Visit Bates' Web site at http://www.batesinfo.com for extensive information about the business and to read articles she's written. She's also the author of *The Online Deskbook* (Information Today, Inc.) and a quarterly electronic newsletter called *For Your Information*. There's also *Researching Online for Dummies* by Reva Basch (IDG Books Worldwide, 1998).

Employers

A large number of information professionals are employed by colleges, universities, and corporations, and gain experience in full-time staff positions before starting their own businesses. Those who work for themselves contract with a number of different kinds of businesses and organizations. People seeking marketing information make the most use of the services of information professionals. Attorneys, consulting firms, public relations firms, and government agencies also hire researchers. With the Internet, a researcher can work anywhere in the country, serving clients all around the world. However, living in a large city will allow you better access to more expansive public records when performing manual research.

Starting Out

People become researchers through a variety of different routes. You may go into business for yourself after gaining a lot of experience within an industry, such as in aviation or pharmaceuticals. Using your expertise, insider knowledge, and professional connections, you can serve as a consultant on issues affecting the business. Or you may become an independent researcher after working as a special librarian, having developed computer and search skills. The one thing most researchers have in common, however, is extensive experience in finding information and presenting it. Once you have the knowledge necessary to start your own information business, you should take seminars offered by such organizations as the IPI. Amelia Kassel, president and owner of MarketingBase (http://www.marketingbase.com), a successful information brokering company, offers a mentoring program via email. As mentor, she advises on such subjects as online databases, marketing strategies, and pricing.

Before leaving her full-time job, Bates spent a year preparing for her own business. She says, "I didn't want to spend time doing start-up stuff that I could spend marketing or doing paying work." She saved business cards and established contacts (which included joining AIIP). She saved $10,000 and set up a home-based office with a computer, desk, office supplies, fax, and additional phone lines. To help others starting out, Bates has written *Getting Your First Five Clients,* available through AIIP.

Advancement

The first few years of business will be difficult and will require long hours of marketing, promotion, and building a clientele. Advancement will depend on your ability to make connections and to broaden your client base. Some researchers start out specializing in a particular area, such as in telephone research or public record research, before venturing out into different areas. Once you're capable of handling projects from diverse sources, you can expand your business. You can also take on larger projects as you begin to meet other reliable researchers with whom you can join forces.

Earnings

Even if you have a great deal of research experience, your first few years in the business will be lean ones, and you shouldn't be surprised to make less than $20,000. As with any small business, it takes a few years to develop contacts and to spread word of your expertise. Eventually, you should be able to make a salary equivalent to that of a full-time special librarian—a 1997 salary survey by the Special Library Association puts the national median at $45,500. Some very experienced independent researchers with a number of years of self-employment may make over $100,000.

Burwell Enterprises, Inc., which provides services to the information industry, has conducted a salary survey in the past. Helen Burwell, president of Burwell Enterprises, estimates that the average information broker charges $75 an hour. This hourly rate is affected by geographic location, and the broker's knowledge of the subject matter. Information brokers can make more money in cities like New York and Washington, DC, where their services are in higher demand. Also, someone doing high-level patent research, which requires a great deal of expertise, can charge more than someone retrieving public records.

Work Environment

Most independent researchers work out of their own homes. This means they have a lot of control over their environment, but it also means they're always close to their workstations. As a result, you may find yourself working longer hours than if you had an outside office and a set weekly schedule. "This is easily a 50- to 60-hour a week job," Bates says. As your own boss, your work isn't closely supervised, but you may work as a team with other researchers and consultants on some projects. You'll also be discussing the project with your clients both before and after you've begun your research. Although a lot of your work will be at the computer, you'll have to make trips to libraries, government offices, and other places that hold information that's not available online.

Outlook

Burwell anticipates that independent information professionals will continue to find a great deal of work, but the growth of the industry won't be as rapid as in the past. Between 1984 and 1990, the industry grew by 20 percent, attributable to the development of research and online technology. The 1998 edition of *The Burwell World Directory of Information Brokers* listed fewer professionals than the 1995 edition, but 1998 is the first year that a fee was required for listing. Based on numbers listed in the 1995 edition, the industry has probably grown to approximately 2,000 independent information professionals in the United States.

The Internet is making it easier for people and businesses to conduct their own online research; this is expected to help business for online researchers rather than hurt. Alex Kramer, president of the AIIP, predicts that the more people recognize the vast amount of information available to them, the more they'll seek out the assistance of online researchers to efficiently compile that information.

As the Internet expands, and more documents become regularly available, information brokers will be relying even more on the Internet for both compiling and delivering information. Online researchers are also subject to the expense and availability of online services and databases. If subscribing to online database services becomes too expensive, researchers will have to consider other ways of accessing the services.

For More Information

For information about library science programs and scholarships, contact:

American Library Association (ALA)
50 East Huron
Chicago, IL 60611
Tel: 800-545-2433
Web: http://www.ala.org

To learn more about the benefits of association membership, contact:

Association of Independent Information Professionals
234 West Delaware Avenue
Pennington, NJ 08534
Tel: 609-730-8759
Web: http://www.aiip.org

For information about seminars and books on information brokers, contact:

Information Professionals Institute
3724 FM 1960 West, Suite 214
Houston, TX 77068
Tel: 281-537-8344
Web: http://www.ipi-books.com or http://www.burwellinc.com

For information on continuing education, contact:

Special Libraries Association
1700 18th Street, NW
Washington, DC 20009-2514
Tel: 202-234-4700
Web: http://www.sla.org/

Personal Chefs

Family and Consumer Science Health	School Subjects
Communication/ideas Leadership/management	Personal Skills
Primarily indoors Primarily multiple locations	Work Environment
Some postsecondary training	Minimum Education Level
$35,000 to $42,000 to $50,000	Salary Range
Voluntary	Certification or Licensing
Faster than the average	Outlook

Overview

Personal chefs prepare menus for individuals and their families, purchase the ingredients for the meals, then cook, package, and store the meals in the clients' own kitchens. Approximately 3,000 personal chefs work across the United States and Canada, cooking for busy families, seniors, people with disabilities, and others who don't have the time or the ability to prepare meals for themselves.

History

Since the beginning of time, humans have experimented with food and cooking techniques in efforts to create simpler, quicker, more balanced meals. The development of pottery and agriculture was the earliest step toward better cooking, after years of using skulls and bones as cooking pots and hunting for meat. Cooks have always built from the progress of previous generations; Catherine de Medicis of Italy is often credited with introducing, in the 16th century, masterful cooking to the French where fine cuisine developed into an art form.

Though royalty, the famous, and the wealthy have long hired private chefs to work in their kitchens, personal chefs have only recently come onto the scene. Within the last 10 years, experienced cooks, either looking to expand their catering and restaurant businesses, or burnt-out from working as chefs, have begun meeting the demand for quick, easy meals that taste homemade. Men and women are holding down demanding, time-consuming jobs, and looking for alternatives to microwave dinners, fast food, and frozen pizzas. David MacKay founded the first professional association for personal chefs, the United States Personal Chef Association (USPCA), in 1991, and helps to establish over 400 new businesses every year. The American Personal Chef Institute (APCI), founded by Candy Wallace, has also developed in recent years, offering training materials and certification to experienced cooks wanting to set up their own businesses.

The Job

What will you be cooking for dinner tonight? Spice-rubbed lamb chops with roasted tomatoes? Tarragon chicken with West Indian pumpkin soup? Or maybe turkey parmesan on a bed of red-pepper linguini? If you're rolling up your sleeves and ready to take on a variety of cooking challenges, then a personal chef service may be in your future. People without the time to cook, or without the ability, or those who just plain don't care to cook, are calling upon the services of chefs who will come into their kitchens, throw together delicious meals, then stack the meals in their freezers. A complete meal prepared according to the client's specifications is then only a few minutes of re-heating away.

A personal chef is usually someone with a great deal of cooking experience who, for a per-meal fee, will prepare enough meals to last a few days, or a few weeks, for individuals and their families. As a personal chef, you first meet with a new client to discuss special dietary needs and food preferences. Some clients require vegetarian and low-fat cooking; others have diabetes, or swallowing disorders that require special consideration. (If you have to do a great deal of research into a special diet plan, you might charge an additional consultation fee.) From these specifications, you prepare a menu. On the day that you'll be cooking the meals, you visit the grocery store to purchase fresh meats, fish, fruits, and vegetables. At the home of your client, you prepare the meals, package them, label them, and put them in the freezer.

Depending on the number of meals, you'll spend anywhere from 3 to 8 hours in your client's kitchen. You then clean up after yourself, and move onto your next client. Personal chefs are able to control their work hours by limiting the number of clients they take on. You'll need between 5 and 10 regular clients to earn a full-time wage.

Most personal chefs prepare the meals in the kitchens of the clients, thereby avoiding the requirements of licensing their own kitchens for commercial use. Greg Porter, a personal chef in South Carolina, is an exception to this norm. As the owner of Masterchef Catering, he is able to prepare meals for his clients in his own commercial kitchen. He had been catering for four years when he began reading articles about personal cheffing. "I researched it on the Internet," he says, "and realized that I was already set up to do it."

Greg pursued training from the APCI and branched out into the business of personal chef. An article about him in an area newspaper resulted in five new clients. "I don't know of anyone else doing this in South Carolina," Greg says. He prepares upscale, gourmet meals for his clients. "Salmon," he lists, "fresh steak, duck breast, rack of lamb, baby back ribs."

But cooking isn't the only talent called upon for success in the personal chef business. You must also know meals and ingredients that can be easily frozen and reheated without hurting taste and appearance. You should have an understanding of nutrition, health, and sanitation. Good business sense is also important, as you'll be keeping financial records, marketing your service, and scheduling and billing clients. You'll be testing recipes, experimenting with equipment, and looking for the most cost-effective ways to purchase groceries. "APCI doesn't teach you how to cook," Greg says. "It shows you the ins and outs of the business."

Candy Wallace, the founder of APCI, developed the training course based on her own experiences as owner of "The Serving Spoon," a personal chef service. "The course is about personalizing service," she says, "as well as personalizing business to support your own well-being." Candy has been in the business for five years. "I started by taking care of the little old ladies in my neighborhood," she says, referring to how she would drive elderly neighbors to their doctors' appointments, run errands for them, and help them prepare meals. She realized she could expand these services. She knew many people longing for the quality and nutrition of a home-cooked meal, but with the ease and speed of the less-healthy, chemical-laden frozen dinners. "I decided to design a program," she says, "for busy corporate women who didn't want their children to glow in the dark."

Most personal chefs try to confine their services to their local areas, or neighborhoods, to keep travel from kitchen to kitchen at a minimum. Sometimes, a good personal chef's services become so valuable to a client, the chef will be invited along on a family's vacation. "I've gone with clients to Palm Springs, Tahoe, Maui . . . .," Candy says.

Requirements

High School

A home economics course can give you a good taste of what it's like to be a personal chef. You'll learn something about cooking, budgeting for groceries, and how to use various cooking equipment and appliances. A course in health will teach you about nutrition and a proper diet. Take a business course that offers lessons in bookkeeping and accounting to help you prepare for the record-keeping aspect of the job. A composition or communications course can help you develop the writing skills you'll need for self-promotion. Join a business organization for the chance to meet with small business owners, and to learn about the fundamentals of business operation.

Postsecondary Training

Both the APCI and the USPCA offer self-study courses and seminars on the personal chef business. These courses are not designed to teach people how to cook, but rather how to start a service, how to market it, how much to charge for services, and other concerns specific to the personal chef business. These courses also offer recipes for foods that freeze and store well. The USPCA has begun to accredit community colleges that offer personal chef courses as part of a culinary curriculum.

A formal education isn't required of personal chefs, but a good culinary school can give you valuable cooking experience. "You must be well trained," Greg advises. Greg holds an associate degree in the culinary arts from the Johnson and Wales Culinary Institute, one of the highest ranked cooking schools in the country. With a degree, you can pursue work in restaurants, hotels, health care facilities, and other industries needing the expertise of professional cooks. Culinary programs include courses in vegetarian cooking, menu design, food safety and sanitation, along with courses like economics and math. "But what will teach you more," Greg says, "is working part-time for a restaurant, or a caterer, to learn the business. I've sold food, catered, managed, owned a restaurant—I've done it all, to learn the whole business inside out."

Certification or Licensing

To become a Certified Personal Chef (CPC) with the USPCA, you must work for at least three months as a personal chef. You're required to complete written and practical exams, and submit testimonial letters from at least five different clients. The APCI also offers certification to those who complete their special training course. One quarter to one half of the personal chefs working in the United States and Canada are certified, but certification isn't required to work in the business.

Because you'll be working in the kitchens of your clients, you won't need licensing, or to adhere to the health department regulations of commercial kitchens. A few states, however, do charge permit fees, and require some inspections of the vehicle in which you carry groceries and cooking equipment.

Other Requirements

Greg emphasizes that a person should have an outgoing personality to be successful as a personal chef. "Customer service is the most important thing," he says. "If you're not people-oriented, you can just hang it up." A strong work ethic and an ambition to succeed are also very important—you'll be promoting your business, building a client list, and handling administrative details all by yourself. You'll need patience, too, not only as you prepare quality meals, but as you wait for your business to develop and your client list to grow. You should be a creative thinker, capable of designing interesting menus within the specifications of the client. And, of course, keep in mind that you'll be cooking several meals a day, every day. So it may not be enough to just "like" cooking; you'll need a passion for it.

Exploring

The most valuable exploration you can do is to spend time in the kitchen. Learn how to properly use the cooking appliances and utensils. Experiment with recipes; various Web posting sites include recipes that are good to freeze and store. This way you'll learn what meals would work best in a personal chef service. Cook for friends and family, and volunteer to work at high school banquets and soup dinners. Contact the professional associations for names of personal chefs in your area. Some chefs participate in mentoring programs to help people learn about the business. Look into part-time work with a restaurant, cafe, or caterer. Many caterers hire assistants on a temporary basis to help with large events.

Employers

As a personal chef, you'll be in business for yourself. Nearly all personal chef services are owned and operated by individuals, though some well-established chefs serving a largely populated, affluent area may hire assistants. If you live in one of these areas and have some cooking experience and education, you may be able to hire on as a cook with a big personal chef operation. But you'll most likely be in business for yourself and will promote your services in areas near your home.

The majority of people who use the services of personal chefs are working couples who have household incomes of over $70,000. Most of these couples have children. Personal chefs also work for people with disabilities and senior citizens. "A lot of clients are seniors," Candy Wallace of APCI says. "They want to stay in their own homes, but never want to see the inside of a grocery store or a kitchen again. Some of these clients are in their 90s."

Starting Out

David MacKay, executive director and founder of USPCA, emphasizes that the career of personal chef is really for those who have tried other careers and have some experience in the food and service industry. The new personal chef courses being offered by USPCA-accredited community colleges may eventually change this and may attract people with little cooking experience into the business. For now, though, a personal chef course and seminar isn't really enough to get you started unless you also have a culinary education, or a great deal of knowledge about cooking.

If you feel confident that you have the cooking knowledge necessary to prepare good-tasting, well-balanced meals for paying customers, then you should consider training through either APCI or USPCA. Once you have a good sense of the requirements and demands of the job, you can start seeking out clients. Because you'll be cooking with the stoves and appliances of your clients, you don't need to invest much money into starting up your business. An initial investment of about $1,000 will buy you some quality cookware and utensils. But you'll also need a reliable vehicle, as you'll be driving to the grocery store and to the homes of your clients every day.

Volunteer your services for a week or two to friends and neighbors who you think might be interested in hiring you. Print up some fliers and cards, and post your name on community bulletin boards. You may have to offer a low, introductory price to entice clients to try your services.

Advancement

Most personal chefs only cook for 1 or 2 clients every day, so maintaining between 5 and 10 clients will keep you pretty busy. If you're able to attract many more customers than you can handle, it may benefit you to hire assistants and to raise your prices. As you advance in the business, you may choose to expand into other areas, like catering large events, writing food-related articles for a local newspaper or magazine, or teaching cooking classes. You may also meet with owners of grocery stores and restaurants, consulting with them about developing their own meal take-out services.

Earnings

According to the USPCA, salaries for personal chefs range from about $35,000 annually on the low end to $50,000 on the high end. Some chefs with assistant cooks and a number of clients can make much more than that, but businesses composed of a single owner/operator average about $40,000 per year.

Personal chefs usually sell their services as a package deal-typically $250 to $300 for 10 meals for 2 people, with a fee of $10 to $15 for each additional meal. A complete package may take a full day to prepare. This may seem like a very good wage, but it's important to remember that you're also paying for the groceries. Though you'll be able to save some money by buying staples in bulk, and by planning your menus efficiently, you'll also be spending a lot on fresh meat, fish, and vegetables. One-third or less of your 10-meal package fee will go toward the expense of its ingredients.

Work Environment

Greg likes the "personal" aspect of working as a personal chef. "My customers become friends," he says. He appreciates being able to prepare meals based on the individual tastes of his customers, rather than "the 300 people coming into a restaurant." Many personal chefs enter the business after burning out on the demands of restaurant work. As a personal chef, you can make your own schedule, avoiding the late nights, long hours, and weekends of restaurant service.

Though you won't be working in your own home, there isn't much travel involved. You will have to visit a grocery store every morning for fresh meats and produce, but most of the hours of each work day will be spent in one kitchen. Freezer space, pantries, and stoves obviously won't be as large as those in a commercial kitchen, but your work spaces will be much more inviting and homey than those in the back of a restaurant. Your work will be done entirely on your own, with little supervision by your clients. In most cases, your clients will be at work, allowing you to create your meals, and your messes, in private.

Outlook

The personal chef industry is growing in leaps and bounds, and will continue to do so. The career has become recognized by culinary institutes, and some schools are beginning to include personal chef courses as part of their curriculums. The USPCA predicts that the personal chef industry will contribute over $100 million a year to the U.S. economy by the early 21st century. The national publications *Entrepreneur Magazine, Business Start-ups, US*

News and World Report, and others have listed personal chef services as one of the hottest new businesses.

Though the basics of the job will likely remain the same in future years, it is subject to some trends. You will need to keep up with diet fads and new health concerns, as well as trends in gourmet cooking. As the career gains prominence, states may regulate it more rigorously, requiring certain health inspections and permits. Some states may also begin to require special food safety and sanitation training.

For More Information

The USPCA offers training courses, certification, and mentorship:

United States Personal Chef Association
3615 Highway 528, Suite 107
Albuquerque, NM 87114-8919
Tel: 505-899-4223 and 800-995-2138
Web: http://www.uspca.com

The APCI holds seminars, offers a self-study course, and maintains an informative Web site with a personal chef message board:

American Personal Chef Institute
4572 Delaware Street
San Diego, CA 92116
Tel: 800-644-8389
Web: http://www.personalchef.com

Personal Shoppers

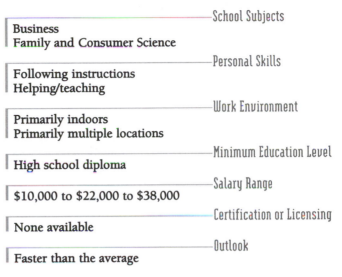

School Subjects
Business
Family and Consumer Science

Personal Skills
Following instructions
Helping/teaching

Work Environment
Primarily indoors
Primarily multiple locations

Minimum Education Level
High school diploma

Salary Range
$10,000 to $22,000 to $38,000

Certification or Licensing
None available

Outlook
Faster than the average

Overview

People who don't have the time or the ability to go shopping for clothes, gifts, groceries, and other items use the services of *personal shoppers*. Personal shoppers shop department stores, look at catalogs, and surf the Internet for the best buys and most appropriate items for their clients. Relying on a sense of style and an ability to spot a bargain, a personal shopper helps clients develop a wardrobe and find gifts for friends, relatives, and employees. Though personal shoppers work all across the country, their services are in most demand in large, metropolitan areas.

History

For decades, American retailers have been working to create easier ways to shop. Mail-order was an early innovation—catalog companies like Montgomery Wards and Sears and Roebuck started business in the late 19th century to meet the shopping needs of people living in rural areas and small towns. Many consumers relied on mail-order for everything from suits and dresses to furniture and stoves; Sears even sold automobiles through the mail. Shopping for food, clothes, and gifts was considered a household chore, a responsibility that belonged to women. By the late 1800s, shopping had developed into a popular past-time in metropolitan areas. Wealthy women of leisure turned downtown shopping districts into the busiest sections of their cities, as department stores, boutiques, tea shops, and cafes evolved to serve them.

As more women joined the work force after World War II, retailers worked to make their shopping areas more convenient. Supermarkets, shopping centers, and malls became popular. Toward the end of the 20th century, shoppers began looking for even more simplicity and convenience. In the 1990s, many companies began to market their products via the Internet. In addition to Internet commerce, overworked men and women are turning to personal shoppers, professional organizers, and personal assistants to fulfill their shopping needs.

The Job

Looking for a job where you get to shop all the time, tell people what to wear, and spend somebody else's money? Though this may seem to describe the life of the personal shopper, it's not quite accurate. For one thing, you don't get to shop all the time—you will be spending some time in stores and browsing catalogs, but you're often looking for something very specific, and working as quickly as you can. And you're not so much telling people what to wear, as teaching them how to best match outfits, what colors suit them, and what styles are most appropriate for their workplaces. And, yes, you're spending someone else's money, but it's all for someone else's closet.

So, if you're not too disillusioned, read on: working as a personal shopper may still be right for you. As a personal shopper, you help people who are unable or uninterested in doing their own shopping. You'll be hired to look for that perfect gift for a difficult-to-please aunt. You'll be hired by senior citizens, or people with disabilities, to do their grocery shopping and run other shopping errands. You'll help professionals create a nice, complete wardrobe. All the while, you'll rely on your knowledge of the local marketplace in order to do the shopping quickly and efficiently.

Some personal shoppers use their backgrounds in other areas to assist clients. Someone with a background in real estate may serve as a personal shopper for houses, working for a buyer rather than a seller. These house shoppers inspect houses and do some of the client's bargaining. Those with a background in cosmetology may work as *image consultants,* advising clients on their hair, clothes, and make-up. Another shopper may have some experience in dealing antiques, and will help clients locate particular items. An interior decorator may shop for furniture and art to decorate a home.

If you're offering wardrobe consultation, you'll need to visit the client's home and evaluate his or her clothes. You'll help your clients determine what additional clothes and accessories they'll need, and you'll advise them on what jackets to wear with what pants, what skirt to wear with what blouse. Together with the client, you'll determine what additional clothes are needed to complete the wardrobe, and you'll come up with a budget. Then it's off to the stores.

Irene Kato owns I Kan Do It, a personal shopping service. She offers a variety of services, including at-home wardrobe consultation, closet organization, and gift-shopping. "Most of my shopping so far has been for clothes," Irene says. "I have a fairly good idea of what I'm looking for so I don't spend too much time in any one store if I don't see what I want right away. I can usually find two or three choices for my client and rarely have to shop another day." Irene spends about two to three hours every other day shopping, and spends about two hours a day in her office working on publicity, her budget, and corresponding with clients. Shopping for one client can take about three hours. "I have always enjoyed shopping," Irene says, "and especially like finding bargains. Waiting in lines, crowds, etc. do not bother me."

As a personal shopper, you'll likely cater to professionals needing business attire and wardrobe consultation. A smaller part of your business will be shopping for gifts. You may even supplement your business by running non-shopping errands, such as purchasing theater tickets, making deliveries, and going to the post office. Many personal shoppers also work as *professional organizers*: they go into homes and offices to organize desks, kitchens, and closets.

In addition to the actual shopping, you'll have administrative responsibilities. You'll do record-keeping, make phone calls, and schedule appointments. Self-promotion will be very important; because personal shopping is a fairly new endeavor, you have the added burden of educating the public about the service. "A personal shopper has no commodity to sell," Irene says, "only themselves. So it is twice as hard to attract clients." To publicize her business, Irene maintains a Web site that lists the services she provides and testimonials from clients. She also belongs to two professional organizations that help her network and develop her business: Executive Women International (EWI) and Giving Referrals to Other Women (GROW).

Requirements

High School

Take classes in home economics to develop budget and consumer skills, as well as learn about fashion and home design. If the class offers a sewing unit, you'll learn about tailoring, and can develop an eye for clothes sizes. Math, business, and accounting courses will prepare you for the administrative details of the job. English composition and speech classes will help you develop the communication skills you'll need for promoting your business, and for advising clients about their wardrobes.

Postsecondary Training

Many people working as personal shoppers have had experience in other areas of business. They've worked as managers in corporations or have worked as salespeople in retail stores. But because of the entrepreneurial nature of the career, you don't need any specific kind of education or training. A small-business course at your local community college, along with classes in design, fashion, and consumer science, can help you develop the skills you'll need for the job. If you're unfamiliar with the computer, you should take some classes to learn desktop publishing programs for creating business cards and other publicity material.

Other Requirements

"I seem to have an empathy for people," Irene says. "After talking with a client I know what they want and what they're looking for. I am a very good listener." In addition to these people skills, a personal shopper should be patient, and capable of dealing with the long lines and customer service of department stores. You should be creative, and able to come up with a variety of gift ideas. A sense of style is important, along with knowledge of the latest brands and designers. You'll need a good eye for colors and fabrics. You should also be well-dressed and organized so that your client will know to trust your wardrobe suggestions.

Exploring

If you've spent any time at the mall, you probably already have enough shopping experience. And if you've had to buy clothes and gifts with limited funds, then you know something about budgeting. Sign up for the services of a personal shopper in a department store; in most stores the service is free, and you'll get a sense of how a shopper works. Pay close attention to the information they request from you in the beginning, then ask them later about their decision-making process. Irene advises future personal shoppers to work a few years at a retail clothing store. "This way," she says, "you can observe the way people dress, what shapes and sizes we all are, how fashion trends come and go, and what stays."

Employers

Most of your clients will be professional men and women with high incomes and busy schedules. You'll be working with people with new jobs requiring dress clothes, but also with people who need to perk up an old wardrobe. You may work for executives in corporations who need to buy gifts for large staffs of employees. Some of your clients may be elderly or have disabilities and have problems getting out to do their shopping.

Starting Out

The start-up costs can be very low; you may only have to invest in a computer, business cards, and a reliable form of transportation. But it could take you a very long time to develop a regular clientele. You'll want to develop the business part-time while still working full-time at another, more reliable job. Some of your first clients may come from your workplace—offer free introductory services to a few people and encourage them to spread the word around and hand out your business card. You'll also need to become very familiar with the local retail establishments and the discount stores with low-cost, high-quality merchandise.

"My friends and colleagues at work," Irene says, "were always complimentary on what I wore and would ask where I bought my clothes, where they could find certain items, where were the best sales." Irene was taking the part-time approach to developing her personal shopping service, when downsizing at her company thrust her into the new business earlier than she'd planned. She had the opportunity to take an entrepreneur class at a local private university which helped her devise a business plan and taught her about the pros and cons of starting a business.

Advancement

The first few years of your personal shopper business will likely be lean. After a few years of working part-time, you may be able to turn it into a well-paying, full-time job for yourself. As more people learn about your business, you'll take on more clients. Eventually, you may be able to hire an assistant to help you with the administrative work, such as client billing and scheduling.

Earnings

Personal shoppers bill their clients in different ways: you'll set a regular fee for services, charge a percentage of the sale, or charge an hourly rate. You might use all these methods in your business; your billing method may depend on the client and the service. For example, when offering wardrobe consultation and shopping for clothes, you may find it best to charge by the hour; when shopping for a small gift, it may be more reasonable to only charge a percentage. Personal shoppers charge anywhere from $25 to $125 an hour; the average hourly rate is about $75. Successful shoppers living in a large city can make between $1,500 and $3,000 a month.

Work Environment

You'll have all the advantages of owning your own business, including setting your own hours, and keeping a flexible schedule. But you'll also have all the disadvantages, such as job insecurity and lack of benefits. "I have a bad habit of thinking about my business almost constantly," Irene says. Though you won't have to deal with the stress of a full-time office job, you will have the stress of finding new clients and keeping the business afloat entirely by yourself.

Your office will be in your home, but you'll be spending a lot of time with people, from clients to salespeople. You'll obviously spend some time in department stores; if you like to shop, this can be enjoyable even when you're not buying anything for yourself. In some cases, you'll be visiting client's homes to advise them on their wardrobe. You can expect to do a lot of traveling, driving to a department store after a meeting with a client, then back to the clients with the goods.

Outlook

Personal shopping is a new business development, so anyone embarking on the career will be taking some serious risks. There's not a lot of research available about the career, no national professional organization specifically serving personal shoppers, and no real sense of the career's future. The success of Internet commerce will probably have a big effect on the future of personal shopping. If purchasing items through the Internet becomes more commonplace, personal shoppers may have to establish places for themselves on the World Wide Web. Some personal shoppers currently with Web sites offer consultation via email and help people purchase products online.

It may be in your best interest to offer as expansive a service as you can. Professional organizing is being recognized as one of the top home businesses for the future; the membership for the National Association of Professional Organizers (NAPO) has doubled every year since 1985. *Personal assistants,* those who run errands for others, have also caught the attention of industry experts, and there are programs to help you get started as an assistant.

For More Information

To learn about the career of professional organizer, contact:

National Association of Professional Organizers
1033 La Posada, Suite 220
Austin, TX 78752
Tel: 512-206-0151
Web: http://www.napo.net

To learn about a program that can help you establish a business as a personal assistant, contact:

Personal Assistants International
1800 30th Street, Suite 220C
Boulder, CO 80301
Tel: 303-443-7646
Web: http://www.personalassistants.com

Personal Trainers

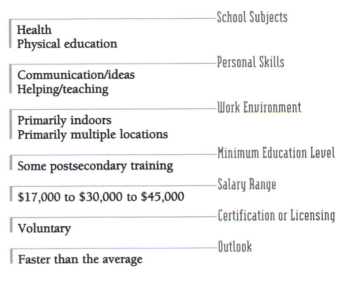

	School Subjects
Health Physical education	
	Personal Skills
Communication/ideas Helping/teaching	
	Work Environment
Primarily indoors Primarily multiple locations	
	Minimum Education Level
Some postsecondary training	
	Salary Range
$17,000 to $30,000 to $45,000	
	Certification or Licensing
Voluntary	
	Outlook
Faster than the average	

Overview

Personal trainers, often known as *fitness trainers,* assist health-conscious people with exercise, weight training, weight loss, diet and nutrition, and medical rehabilitation. During one training session, or over a period of several sessions, trainers teach their clients how to achieve their health and fitness goals. They train in the homes of their clients, their own studio spaces, or in health clubs. Approximately 55,000 personal trainers work in the United States, either independently or on the staff of a fitness center.

History

For much of the last half of the 20th century, "98-pound weaklings" were tempted by the Charles Atlas' comic book ads to buy his workout plan and to bulk up. Atlas capitalized on a concern for good health that developed into the fitness industry after World War II. Though physical fitness has always been important to the human body, things have changed quite a bit since the days when people had to chase and hunt their own food. Before the industrial revolution, people were much more active, and the need for supplemental exercise was unnecessary. But the 20th century has brought easier living, laziness, and processed snack foods.

Even as early as the late 1800s, people became concerned about their health and weight and began to flock to spas and exercise camps. This proved to be a passing fad for the most part, but medical and nutritional study began to carefully explore the significance of exercise. During World War II, rehabilitation medicine proved more effective than extended rest in returning soldiers to the front line. Even the early days of TV featured many morning segments devoted to exercise. The videotape revolution of the 1980s went hand in hand with a new fitness craze, as Jane Fonda's workout tape became a bestseller and inspired a whole industry of fitness tapes and books. Now most health clubs offer the services of fitness trainers to attend to the personal health concerns of its members.

The Job

Remember the first time you ever went to the gym? The weight machines resembled medieval forms of torture, and the buff bodybuilders loitered about, as if it was their job to be in better shape than everybody else. So, to avoid the weight training, you stuck to the treadmill, running like a gerbil on caffeine. Or maybe you called upon the services of a personal trainer. If you have worked with a personal trainer, then you've learned a great deal about your own health and fitness: you've learned how to properly use weight machines; you've learned about calisthenics and cardiovascular exercise; you've developed a proper diet for yourself. If you've reached your own workout goals, then you may be ready to help others reach theirs. "You have to believe in working out and eating healthy," advises Emelina Edwards, a personal trainer in New Orleans. For 12 years she's been in the business of personal training, a career she chose after whipping herself into great shape at the age of 46. Now, at 58, she has a lot of first-hand experience in training, nutrition, aerobic exercise, and stress management. Emelina says, "You have to practice what you preach."

And practice, Emelina does—not only does she devote time every day to her own weight training, jogging, and meditation, but she works with 3 to 5 clients in the workout facility in her home. She has a total of about 20 clients, some of whom she assists in one-on-one sessions, and others in small groups. Her clients have included men and women from the ages of 20 to 80 who are looking to improve their general physical conditions, or to work on specific ailments. When meeting with a client for the first time, Emelina gets a quick history of physical problems and medical conditions. "If the problems are serious," she says, "I check with their doctor. If mild, I explain to them what I believe will help." When she discovered that 4 out of 5 people seeking her help suffered from back problems, she did a great deal of research on back pain and how to alleviate it through exercise. "I teach people how to do for themselves," she says. "Sometimes I see a person once, or for 3 or 4 sessions, or forever."

In addition to working directly with clients, Emelina is active promoting her line of "Total Body Rejuvenation" products. These products, consisting of audio tapes and books, are based on her years of experience and the many articles she has written for fitness publications. A recent appearance on the popular Spanish talk show "Christina" has resulted in a number of calls that she has had to handle herself. When she's not training clients, writing articles, and selling products, she's reading fitness publications to keep up on the business, as well as speaking at public events. "When I realized I loved training," she says, "I thought of all the things I could relate to it. So along with the training, I began to write about it, and to give talks on health and fitness."

To have a successful career as a personal trainer, you don't necessarily have to keep as busy as Emelina. You may choose to specialize in certain areas of personal training. You may work as an *athletic trainer,* helping athletes prepare for sports activities. You may specialize in helping with the rehabilitation treatment of people with injuries and other physical problems. Yoga, dance, martial arts, boxing, water fitness: these have all become aspects of special training programs. People call upon the aid of personal trainers to help them quit smoking, to assist with healthy pregnancies, and to maintain mental and emotional stability. Whatever the problem, whether mental or physical, people are turning to exercise and nutrition to help them deal with it.

Many personal trainers have their own studios or home gyms where they train their clients; others go into the homes of their clients. Because of the demands of the workplace, many personal trainers also work in offices and corporate fitness centers. Though most health clubs hire their own trainers to assist with club members, some hire freelance trainers as independent contractors. These independent contractors are not considered staff members and don't receive employee benefits. (IDEA, a fitness professional association, found that 30 percent of the personal trainers hired by the fitness centers surveyed were independent contractors.)

Requirements

High School

If you're interested in health and fitness, you're probably already taking physical education classes and involved in sports activities. It's also important to take health courses and courses like home economics, which include lessons in diet and nutrition. Business courses can help you prepare for the management aspect of running your own personal training service. Science courses such as biology, chemistry, and physiology are important for your understanding of muscle groups, food and drug reactions, and other concerns of exercise science. If you're not interested in playing on sports teams, you may be able to volunteer as an assistant—you'll learn about athletic training, as well as rehabilitation treatments.

Postsecondary Training

A college education isn't required to work as a personal trainer, but you can benefit from one of the many fitness-related programs offered at colleges across the country. Some relevant college programs are: health education, exercise and sports science, fitness program management, and athletic training. These programs include courses in therapeutic exercise, nutrition, aerobics, and fitness and aging. IDEA recommends a bachelor's degree from a program that includes at least a semester each in anatomy, kinesiology, and exercise physiology. IDEA has some scholarships available to students seeking careers as fitness professionals.

If you're not interested in a full four-year program, many schools offer shorter versions of their bachelor's programs. Upon completing a shorter program, you'll receive either an associate's degree or certification from the school. Once you've established yourself in the business, continuing education courses are important for you to keep up with the advances in the industry. IDEA is one of many organizations that offer independent study courses, conferences, and seminars.

Certification or Licensing

There are so many schools and organizations that offer certification to personal trainers that it has become a concern in the industry. Without more rigid standards, the profession could suffer at the hands of less experienced, less skilled trainers. Some organizations only require membership fees and short tests for certification. Emelina isn't certified and doesn't believe that certification is necessary. "Experience is what counts," she says.

But some health clubs look for certified trainers when hiring independent contractors. If you are seeking certification, you should choose a certifying board that offers scientifically based exams and requires continuing education credits. American Council on Exercise (ACE), the National Federation of Professional Trainers (NFPT), and American Fitness Professionals and Associates (AFPA) are just a few of the many groups with certification programs.

Other Requirements

Physical fitness and knowledge of health and nutrition are the most important assets of personal trainers. "The more intelligently you can speak to someone," Emelina says, "the more receptive they'll be." Your clients will also be more receptive to patience and friendliness. "I'm very enthusiastic and positive," Emelina says in regards to the way she works with her clients. You should be capable of explaining things clearly, and capable of recognizing progress and encouraging it. You should be comfortable working one-on-one with people of all ages and in all physical conditions. An interest in reading fitness books and publications is important to your continuing education.

Exploring

Your high school may have a weight-training program, or some other extracurricular fitness program, as part of the athletic department—in addition to signing up for the program, assist the faculty who manage it. That way, you can learn about what goes into developing and maintaining such a program. If your school doesn't have a fitness program, seek one out at a community center, or join a health club. You should also try the services of a personal trainer. By conditioning yourself and eating a healthy diet, you'll get a good sense of the duties of a personal trainer. Any number of books and magazines address issues of health and nutrition and offer weight-training advice. A magazine specifically for personal trainers is published 10 times a year by IDEA. Seek out part-time work at a gym or health club, and you'll meet trainers and learn about weight machines and certification programs.

Employers

As a personal trainer, you'll find opportunities to work for all age groups. Individuals hire the services of trainers, as do companies for the benefit of its employees. Though most health clubs hire personal trainers full-time, a large percentage of clubs hire trainers on an independent contractor basis. Sports and exercise programs at community colleges hire trainers part-time to conduct classes.

Personal trainers can find clients in most major cities in all regions of the country. In addition to health clubs and corporate fitness centers, trainers find work at YMCAs, aerobics studios, and hospital fitness centers.

Starting Out

Most people who begin personal training do so after successful experiences with their own training. Once you've developed a good exercise regimen and healthy diet plan for yourself, you may feel ready to help others. Emelina had hit a low point in her life, following a divorce and money problems, and had turned to weight training to help her get through the difficult times. "I didn't have a college degree," she says, "and I needed something to do. All I had was weight training." She then called up all the women she knew, promoting her services as a personal trainer. Through the benefit of word-of-mouth, Emelina built up a clientele.

Some trainers begin by working part-time or full-time for health clubs and, after making connections, they go into business for themselves. As with most small businesses, personal trainers must promote themselves through classified ads, fliers posted in community centers, and other forms of advertisement. Many personal trainers have published guides on how to establish businesses. IDEA offers a package called "The Business of Personal Training," which includes a textbook and audio cassettes with advice on selling and marketing services, developing networking skills, and creating partnerships with retailers, medical professionals, and others.

Advancement

After you've taken on as many individual clients as you need to maintain a business, you may choose to lead small group training sessions or conduct large aerobics classes. Some trainers join forces with other trainers to start their own fitness centers. Emelina has advanced her business by venturing out into other areas of fitness instruction, such as publishing books and speaking to groups. "I want to develop more in the public speaking arena," she says. Right now, she only speaks to local groups—she'd like to go national. "I'd also like to break into the Latin market," she says. "The interest is there, and the response has been great."

Earnings

A compensation survey conducted by IDEA in 1997 listed the wages of personal trainers who worked as independent contractors for health clubs and other fitness centers. Over one-half of the trainers earned an hourly wage of $20 to $29.99, with 26 percent receiving $30 or over. As for average yearly salary, 57 percent received $20,000 to $29,999, 29 percent received $15,000 to $19,999, and 14 percent received $40,000 and over. Most independent contractors are paid by the hour, according to the survey, and the top three factors determining pay are certification, continuing education, and years in the industry. Working with your own clients in your own home, you can charge a higher hourly rate. The average hourly fee for the services of personal trainers is $40 to $50.

Work Environment

Personal training is obviously a physically demanding job; but, if you're in good shape and eating the right foods, you should be able to easily handle the demands. Because you'll be working out of your home, your work environment and comfort is under your control. Working in a gym as an independent contractor will also provide a comfortable workplace. Most good gyms maintain a cool temperature, keep the facilities clean and well-lit, and care for the weight machines. Whether in a gym or at home, you'll be working directly with your clients, usually in one-on-one training sessions. In this teaching situation, you'll want to keep the workplace quiet and conducive to learning. Exercise as stress management is what many of your clients will be seeking, so most of your training will be calm and soothing.

As with most self-employment, sustaining your own business can be both rewarding and difficult. Many trainers appreciate being able to keep their own hours, and to work as little, or as much, as they care to. By setting their own schedules, they can arrange time for their personal workout routines. But, without an employer, there's less security, no benefits, and no steady paycheck. You also have to regularly promote your services and take on new clients.

Outlook

IDEA estimates that there was a 100 percent growth in the business of fitness training between 1997 and 1998. This growth will likely continue, and it's why *Working At Home Magazine* listed fitness training as one of the "Best Businesses for Unique Talents" in their ranking of the top 20 home businesses.

As the baby boomers grow older, so will the clientele of personal trainers. Boomers have long been interested in health and fitness, and they'll carry this into their old age. A knowledge of special weight training, stretching exercises, and diets for seniors will be necessary for personal trainers in the years to come. Trainers will actively promote their services to senior centers and retirement communities.

With the number of health publications and fitness centers, people are much more knowledgeable about exercise and nutrition. This could increase business for personal trainers as people better understand the necessity of proper training and seek out professional assistance. Trainers may also be going into more of their clients' homes as people set up their own workout stations complete with weights and treadmills. In the health and medical field, new developments are constantly affecting how people eat and exercise. As a trainer, you must keep up on these advances, as well as any new trends in fitness and dieting.

For More Information

For information about the fitness industry in general, and personal training specifically, contact IDEA. IDEA conducts surveys, provides continuing education, and publishes a number of books and magazines relevant to the business.

IDEA Health and Fitness Source
6190 Cornerstone Court East, Suite 204
San Diego, CA 92121-3773
Tel: 800-999-4332, ext. 7
Web: http://www.ideafit.com

For general health and fitness topics, and to learn about certification, contact:

American Council on Exercise (ACE)
5820 Oberlin Drive, Suite 102
San Diego, CA 92121-3787
Tel: 619-535-8227
Web: http://www.acefitness.org

Pet Sitters

Business **Family and Consumer Science**	School Subjects
Helping/teaching **Following instructions**	Personal Skills
Indoors and outdoors **Primarily multiple locations**	Work Environment
High school diploma	Minimum Education Level
$5,000 to $20,000 to $40,000	Salary Range
Voluntary	Certification or Licensing
Faster than the average	Outlook

Overview

When pet owners are on vacation or working long hours, they hire *pet sitters* to come to their homes and visit their animals. During short, daily visits, pet sitters feed the animals, play with them, clean up after them, give them medications when needed, and let them in and out of the house for exercise. *Dog walkers* may be responsible only for taking their clients' pets out for exercise. Pet sitters may also be available for overnight stays, looking after the houses of clients as well as their pets.

History

Animals have been revered by humans for centuries, as is evidenced by early drawings on the walls of caves and tombs—cats were even considered sacred by the ancient Egyptians. Though these sacred cats may have had their own personal caretakers, it has only been within the last 10 years that pet sitting has evolved into a successful industry and a viable career option. Before groups such as the National Association of Professional Pet Sitters (NAPPS), which formed in the early 1980s, and Pet Sitters International (PSI) were developed, pet sitting was regarded as a way for people with spare time to make a little extra money on the side. Like babysitting, pet sitting attracted primarily teenagers and women; many children's books over the last century have depicted the trials and tribulations of young entrepreneurs in the business of pet sitting and dog walking. Patti Moran, the founder of both NAPPS and PSI, and author of *Pet Sitting for Profit*, is credited with helping pet sitters gain recognition as successful small business owners. Though many people still only pet sit occasionally for neighbors and friends, others are developing long lists of clientele and proving strong competition to kennels and boarding facilities.

The Job

If you live in a big city, you've seen them hit the streets with their packs of dogs. Dragged along by four or five leashes, the pet sitter walks the dogs down the busy sidewalks, allowing the animals their afternoon exercise while the pet owners are stuck in the office. You may not have realized it, but those dog walkers are probably the owners of thriving businesses. Though a hobby for some, pet sitting is for others a demanding career with many responsibilities. Michele Finley is one of these pet sitters, in the Park Slope neighborhood of Brooklyn, New York. "A lot of people seem to think pet sitting is a walk in the park (pun intended)," she says, "and go into it without realizing what it entails (again)."

For those who can't bear to leave their dogs or cats at kennels or boarders while they are away, pet sitters offer peace of mind to the owners, as well as their pets. With a pet sitter, pets can stay in familiar surroundings, as well as avoid the risks of illnesses passed on by other animals. The pets are also assured routine exercise and no disruptions in their diets. Most pet sitters prefer to work only with cats and dogs, but pet sitters are also called upon to care for birds, reptiles, gerbils, fish, and other animals.

With their own set of keys, pet sitters let themselves into the homes of their clients and care for their animals while they're away at work or on vacation. Pet sitters feed the animals, make sure they have water, and give them their medications. They clean up any messes the animals have made and clean litter boxes. They give the animals attention, playing with them, letting them outside, and taking them for walks. Usually, a pet sitter can provide pet owners with a variety of personal pet care services—they may take a pet to the vet, offer grooming, sell pet-related products, and give advice. Some pet sitters take dogs out into the country, to mountain parks, or to lakes, for exercise in wide-open spaces. "You should learn to handle each pet as an individual," Finley advises. "Just because Fluffy likes his ears scratched doesn't mean Spot does."

Pet sitters typically plan one to three visits (of 30 to 60 minutes in length) per day, or they may make arrangements to spend the night. In addition to caring for the animals, pet sitters also look after the houses of their clients. They bring in the newspapers and the mail; they water the plants; they make sure the house is securely locked. Pet sitters generally charge by the hour or per visit. They may also have special pricing for overtime, emergency situations, extra duties, and travel.

Most pet sitters work alone, without employees, no matter how demanding the work. Though this means getting to keep all the money, it also means keeping all the responsibilities. A successful pet sitting service requires a fair amount of business management. Finley works directly with the animals from 10:00 AM until 5:00 or 6:00 PM, with no breaks; upon returning home, she will have five to 10 phone messages from clients. Part of her evening then consists of scheduling and rescheduling appointments, offering advice on feeding, training, and other pet care concerns, and giving referrals for boarders and vets. But despite these hours, and despite having to work holidays, as well as days when she's not feeling well, Michele appreciates many things about the job. "Being with the furries all day is the best," she says. She also likes not having to dress up for work and not having to commute to an office.

Requirements

As a pet sitter, you'll be running your own business all by yourself; therefore you should take high school courses such as accounting, marketing, and office skills. Computer science will help you learn about the software you'll need for managing accounts and scheduling. Join a school business group that will introduce you to business practices and local entrepreneurs.

Science courses such as biology and chemistry, as well as health courses, will give you some good background for developing animal care skills. As a pet sitter, you'll be overseeing the health of the animals, their exercise, and their diets. You'll also be preparing medications and administering eye and ear drops.

As a high school student, you can easily gain hands-on experience as a pet sitter. If you know anyone in your neighborhood with pets, volunteer to care for the animals whenever the owners go on vacation. Once you've got experience and a list of references, you may even be able to start a part-time job for yourself as a pet sitter.

Many pet sitters start their own businesses after having gained experience in other areas of animal care. Vet techs and pet shop workers may promote their animal care skills to develop a clientele for more profitable pet sitting careers. Graduates from a business college may recognize pet sitting as a great way to start a business with little overhead. But neither a vet tech qualification nor a business degree is required to become a successful pet sitter. And the only special training you need to pursue is actual experience. A local pet shop or chapter of the ASPCA may offer seminars in various aspects of animal care; the NAPPS offers a mentorship program, as well as a newsletter, while PSI sponsors correspondence programs. There are many publications devoted to pet care, such as *Dog Fancy* and *Cat Watch*, which can educate you about pet health and behavior.

PSI offers accreditation on four levels: *Pet Sitting Technician*, *Advanced Pet Sitting Technician*, *Master Professional Pet Sitter*, and *Accredited Pet Sitting Service*. Pet sitters receive accreditation upon completing home study courses in such subjects as animal nutrition, office procedures, and management. Because the accreditation program was developed only within the last few years, PSI estimates that less than 10 percent of pet sitters working today are accredited. That number is likely to increase, though there are no plans for any kind of government regulation that would require accreditation. "I really don't think such things are necessary," Michele says about accreditation. "All you need to know can be learned by working for a good sitter and reading pet health and behavioral newsletters."

Though there is no particular pet-sitting license required of pet sitters, insurance protection is important. Liability insurance protects the pet sitter from lawsuits; both NAPPS and PSI offer group liability packages to its members. Pet sitters must also be bonded. Bonding assures the pet owners that if anything is missing from their homes after a pet sitting appointment, they can receive compensation immediately.

You must love animals and animals must love you. But this love for animals can't be your only motivation—keep in mind that, as a pet sitter, you'll be in business for yourself. You won't have a boss to give you assignments, and you won't have a secretary or bookkeeper to do the paperwork. You also won't have employees to take over on weekends, holidays, and days when you're not feeling well. Though some pet sitters are successful enough to afford assistance, most must handle all the aspects of their businesses by themselves. So, you should be self-motivated, and as dedicated to the management of your business as you are to the animals.

Pet owners are entrusting you with the care of their pets and their homes, so you must be trustworthy and reliable. You should also be organized and prepared for emergency situations. And not only must you be patient with the pets and their owners, but also with the development of your business: it will take a few years to build up a good list of clients.

As a pet sitter, you must also be ready for the dirty work—you'll be cleaning litter boxes and animal messes within the house. On dog walks, you'll be picking up after them on the street. You may be giving animals medications. You'll also be cleaning aquariums and bird cages.

"Work for an established pet sitter to see how you like it," Finley advises. "It's a very physically demanding job and not many can stand it for long on a full-time basis." Pet sitting isn't for those who just want a nine-to-five desk job. Your day will be spent moving from house to house, taking animals into backyards, and walking dogs around the neighborhoods. Though you may be able to develop a set schedule for yourself, you really will have to arrange your work hours around the hours of your clients. Some pet sitters start in the early morning hours, while others only work afternoons or evenings. To stay in business, a pet sitter must be prepared to work weekends, holidays, and long hours in the summertime.

Exploring

There are many books, newsletters, and magazines devoted to pet care. *Pet Sitting for Profit*, by Patti Moran, and *The Professional Pet Sitter* by Lori and Scott Mangold, are a few of the books that can offer insight into pet sitting as a career. Magazines such as *Cat Fancy* can also teach you about the requirements of animal care. And there are any number of books discussing the ins and outs of small business ownership.

Try pet sitting for a neighbor or family member to get a sense of the responsibilities of the job. Some pet sitters hire assistants on an independent contractor basis; contact an area pet sitter listed in the phone book or with one of the professional organizations, and see if you can "hire on" for a day or two. Not only will you learn firsthand the duties of a pet sitter, but you'll also see how the business is run.

Employers

Nearly all pet sitters are self-employed, although a few may work for other successful pet sitters who have built up a large enough clientele to require help. It takes most pet sitters an appreciable period of time to build up a business substantial enough to make a living without other means of income. However, the outlook for this field is excellent and start-up costs are minimal, making it a good choice for animal lovers who want to work for themselves. For those who have good business sense and a great deal of ambition, the potential for success is good.

Starting Out

You're not likely to find job listings under "pet sitter" in the newspaper. Most pet sitters schedule all their work themselves. However, you may find ads in the classifieds or in weekly community papers, from pet owners looking to hire pet sitters. Some people who become pet sitters have backgrounds in animal care—they may have worked for vets, breeders, or pet shops. These people enter the business with a client list already in hand, having made contacts with many pet owners. But, if you're just starting out in animal care, you need to develop a list of references. This may mean volunteering your time to friends and neighbors, or working very cheaply. If you're willing to actually stay in the house while the pet owners are on vacation, you should be able to find plenty of pet sitting opportunities in the summertime. Post your name, phone number, and availability on the bulletin boards of grocery stores, colleges, and coffee shops around town. Once you've developed a list of references, and have made connections with pet owners, you can start expanding, and increasing your profits.

Advancement

Your advancement will be a result of your own hard work; the more time you dedicate to your business, the bigger the business will become. The success of any small business can be very unpredictable. For some, a business can build very quickly, for others it may take years. Some pet sitters start out part-time, perhaps even volunteering, then may find themselves with enough business to quit their full-time jobs and to devote themselves entirely to pet sitting. Once your business takes off, you may be able to afford an assistant, or an entire staff. Some pet sitters even have franchises across the country. You may even choose to develop your business into a much larger operation, such as a dog day care facility.

Earnings

Pet sitters set their own prices, charging by the visit, the hour, or the week. They may also charge consultation fees, and additional fees on holidays. They may have special pricing plans in place, such as for emergency situations or for administering medications. Depending on the kinds of animals (sometimes pet sitters charge less to care for cats than dogs), pet sitters generally charge between $8 and $15 a visit (with a visit lasting between 30 and 60 minutes). PSI conducted a recent salary survey and discovered that the range was too great to determine a median. Some very successful pet sitters have annual salaries of over $100,000, while others only make $5,000 a year. Though a pet sitter can make a good profit in any area of the country, a bigger city will offer more clients. Pet sitters in their first five years of business are unlikely to make more than $10,000 a year; pet sitters who have had businesses for eight years or more may make more than $40,000 a year.

Work Environment

Some pet sitters prefer to work close to their homes; Michele only walks dogs in her Brooklyn neighborhood. In a smaller town, however, pet sitters have to do a fair amount of driving from place to place. Depending on the needs of the animals, the pet sitter will let the pets outside for play and exercise. Although filling food and water bowls and performing other chores within the house is generally peaceful work, walking dogs on the busy city sidewalks can be stressful. And in the wintertime, you'll spend a fair amount of time out in the inclement weather. "Icy streets are murder," Finley says. "And I don't like dealing with people who hate dogs and are always yelling to the get the dog away from them."

Though you'll have some initial interaction with pet owners when getting house keys, taking down phone numbers, and meeting the pets and learning about their needs, most of your work will be alone with the animals. But you won't be totally isolated; if dog walking in the city, you'll meet other dog owners and other people in the neighborhood.

Outlook

Pet sitting as a small business is expected to skyrocket in the coming years. Most pet sitters charge fees comparable to kennels and boarders, but some charge less. And many pet owners prefer to leave their pets in the house, rather than take the pets to unfamiliar locations. This has all made pet sitting a desirable and cost-effective alternative to other pet care situations. Pet sitters have been successful in cities both large and small. In the last few years, pet sitting has been featured in the *Wall Street Journal* and other national publications; last year, *Woman's Day* magazine listed pet sitting as one of the top-grossing businesses for women. Pet Sitters International has grown 500 percent in the last four years.

Because a pet sitting business requires little money to start up, many more people may enter the business hoping to make a tidy profit. This could lead to heavier competition; it could also hurt the reputation of pet sitting if too many irresponsible and unprepared people run bad businesses. But if pet owners remain cautious when hiring pet sitters, the unreliable workers will have trouble maintaining clients.

For More Information

For career and small business information, as well as general information about pet sitting, contact these organizations:

Pet Sitters International
418 East King Street
King, NC 27021-9163
Tel: 336-983-9222
Web: http://www.petsit.com

National Association of Professional Pet Sitters
1200 G Street, NW, Suite 760
Washington, DC 20005
Tel: 202-393-3317
Web: http://www.petsitters.com

Swimming Pool Servicers

	School Subjects
Chemistry Technical/Shop	
	Personal Skills
Following instructions Technical/scientific	
	Work Environment
Indoors and outdoors Primarily multiple locations	
	Minimum Education Level
High school diploma	
	Salary Range
$18,000 to $32,000 to $50,000	
	Certification or Licensing
Voluntary	
	Outlook
About as fast as the average	

Overview

Swimming pool servicers clean, adjust, and perform minor repairs on swimming pools, hot tubs, and their auxiliary equipment. There are millions of swimming pools across the country in hotels, parks, apartment complexes, health clubs, and other public areas; these public pools are required by law to be regularly serviced by trained technicians. The number of homes with private pools is also increasing every year. The owner of a swimming pool service will also hire and train technicians, schedule and bill clients, and market the business.

History

Swimming is as old as walking and running, and swimming pools date back to the bathhouses in the palaces of ancient Greece. These bathhouses were elaborate spas, complete with steam rooms, saunas, and large pools. But swimming was a popular pastime even among those who didn't have access to bathhouses; many swam in the rivers, oceans, and the lakes of the world. The plagues of medieval Europe made people cautious about swimming in unclean waters, but swimming regained popularity in the 1880s in England. Swimmers swam with their heads above water in a style developed when people were still afraid of the water's contamination. This style changed in the mid-1800s when American Indians introduced an early version of the modern "crawl" to Europe. Swimming in natural spring waters was even recommended as a health benefit, inspiring hospitals and spas to develop around hot springs.

The first modern Olympics held in Athens featured swimming as one of the nine competitions, and swimming as both a sport and a pastime has continued to develop along with the technology of pool maintenance. By the 1960s, the National Swimming Pool Foundation had evolved to support research in pool safety and the education of pool operators.

The Job

With your swimming pool service, you'll travel a regularly scheduled route, visiting several pools a day. You'll be responsible for keeping pools clean and pool equipment operating properly. A pool that routinely receives adequate maintenance develops relatively few expensive problems. Mark Randall owns a pool service business in Malibu, California. "My tools range from a tile brush to a state of the art computer and printer," he says. Mark has two employees, so his day usually starts with phone calls to his crew and customers. "Then I go out and clean a few of the more difficult accounts," he says.

Cleaning is one of the regular duties of pool servicers. Leaves and other debris need to be scooped off the surface of the water with a net on a long pole. To clean beneath the surface, you use a special vacuum cleaner on the pool floor and walls. With stainless steel or nylon brushes, you scrub pool walls and the tiles and gutters around the pool's edge to remove the layer of grit and scum that collects at the water line. You also hose down the pool deck and unclog the strainers that cover the drains.

After the cleaning procedures, you test the bacterial content and pH balance (a measure of acidity and alkalinity) of the water. While the tests are simple and take only a few minutes, they are very important. You take a sample of the pool water in a jar and add a few drops of a testing chemical. This causes the water to change colors, indicating the water's chemical balance. You can then determine the amount of chlorine and other chemicals you should add to make the water safe. The chemicals often used, which include potassium iodide, hydrochloric acid, sodium carbonate, chlorine, and others, can be poured directly into the pool or added through a feeder device in the circulation system. These chemicals, when properly regulated, kill bacteria and algae that grow in water. However, too much of them can cause eye or skin irritation. You must wear gloves and be careful when adding the chemicals since they are dangerous in high concentrations. You must follow the correct procedures for applying these chemicals each time, and keep accurate records of what is added to the pool. The chemical makeup of every pool is different and can change daily or even hourly. Home pools usually have their water tested a few times a week, but large public pools are tested hourly.

You'll also inspect and perform routine maintenance on pool equipment, such as circulation pumps, filters, and heaters. In order to clean a filter, you force water backwards through it to dislodge any dirt and debris that have accumulated. You'll make sure there are no leaks in pipes, gaskets, connections, or other parts. If a drain or pipe is clogged, you use a steel snake, plunger, or other plumber's tools to clear it. You will adjust thermostats, pressure gauges, and other controls to make the pool water comfortable. You may make minor repairs to machinery, fixing or replacing small components. When you think major repairs are necessary, you'll inform the pool owner before beginning to make the repairs.

"An accomplished pool tech," Mark says, "can do a pool in about 20 minutes. Most pool techs would do this from 10 to 20 times a day."

Closing outdoor pools for the winter is a major task for swimming pool servicers in most regions of the country. In the fall, you'll drain the water out of the pool and its auxiliary equipment. Openings into the pool are plugged, and all the pool gear, such as diving boards, ladders, and pumps, is removed, inspected, and stored. The pool is covered with a tarpaulin lashed or weighted in place. In climates where water does not freeze, pools are usually kept full and treated with special chemicals through the winter.

Extra work is also required when a pool is opened in the spring. After the pool is uncovered and the tank and pool deck are swept clean, you inspect the pool for cracks, leaks, loose tiles, and broken lamps. You then repair minor items and make recommendations to the owner about any major work that is necessary, such as painting the interior of the pool. You then clean and install the equipment removed in the fall, such as ladders and diving boards. You test water circulation and heating systems to make sure they are operating properly, and then you fill the pool with water. Once the pool is filled, you test the water and add the proper chemicals to make it safe. Pool servicers keep careful records of the maintenance work they have done so they can inform the company and the customer.

Requirements

High School

Take science courses such as chemistry and biology so you can gain understanding of the chemicals you'll be using. Voc-tech courses with lessons in electrical wiring and motors will help you develop skills for repairing the pool servicing machines and equipment. Bookkeeping and accounting courses can teach you how to keep financial and tax records. You should also learn about spreadsheet and database software programs, as you'll be using computers to maintain files on profits and expenses, customers, equipment, and employees. Join a business club to meet small business owners in your area. Serving as an assistant on a swim team can teach you first-hand about the requirements of maintaining a regulation pool.

Postsecondary Training

You can gain the technical training on the job; by hiring on with a pool service business, you'll learn the basics of pool maintenance within a few months. To prepare yourself for the demands of running your own business, enroll in a small business program at your local community college, or take college courses in sales, math, and accounting. Mark has had college and technical training in various fields, and has worked as a mechanic, data analyst, and has built props for a movie studio. "I had no idea I would end up in the pool business," he says. "Luckily, my background was actually very good training for my current business." He recommends that people interested in pool maintenance take courses in electrical applications, electronics, plumbing, and hydraulics.

Certification and Licensing

Mark believes that certification and licensing are very important to running a professional outfit. He is certified by the health department, has a business license, and belongs to the Independent Pool and Spa Service Organization. Certification is also available from the National Swimming Pool Foundation, and by service franchisers. These programs consist of a set number of classroom hours and a written exam. While certification is not necessarily a requirement, it does indicate that you've reached a certain level of expertise and skill, and can help you promote your business.

Other Requirements

Because you'll often work alone, with minimum supervision, it is important that you have self-discipline and a responsible attitude. Your drive and ambition will determine the success of your business. "Persistence is probably the most important quality," Mark says, in listing necessary personal attributes. He also emphasizes a strong work ethic and good communication skills. You'll also need to keep up with the technology of swimming pool maintenance, staying knowledgeable about new equipment and services available to your clients.

Exploring

A summer or part-time job on the staff of a school, park district, community center, or local health club will provide you with a good opportunity to learn more about servicing swimming pools. Hotels, motels, apartment buildings, and condominium complexes also frequently have pools and may hire summer or part-time workers to service them. Such a job could offer firsthand insight into the duties of swimming pool servicers, as well as help in obtaining full-time employment with a pool maintenance company later. *Aqua Magazine* is a good source of technical information concerning pool service. Contact *Aqua Magazine* for a sample issue, or visit Aqua's Web site (http://www.aquamagazine.com) to read some of the articles it publishes.

Employers

The rate of new pool construction is growing 3 to 4 percent every year. With well over 6 million residential swimming pools in the country, pool service owners can find clients in practically every suburban neighborhood. In addition to servicing residential pools, you'll service the pools of motels, apartment complexes, and public parks. Some franchise opportunities, with companies such as PFS Swimming Pool Services, also exist. These franchisers often offer training, and have an initial investment of under $20,000.

Starting Out

Once you have the training, and the money to invest in equipment, you'll pursue a clientele. This may involve promoting your business through advertising, fliers, and word of mouth. You may be able to get referrals from local pool and spa construction companies. "I started out riding with a friend who worked for a large pool service company," Mark says, "and I learned as much as I could. After that, I found a small route for sale." Mark borrowed money from the bank to buy the established route of customers, then used his training to start servicing pools. "It was sink or swim, pardon the pun," he says. "But I worked very hard the first couple of years and got lucky and have been fairly successful."

Advancement

You'll advance as your business grows. More area pool construction, good word of mouth, and some years in the business will attract more clients and more routes to service. If your business does really well, you may be able to take on employees, allowing you to assign staff members to the service work while you focus on office work and administrative details. You could also expand your business to include the sale of pools, spas, and maintenance equipment. "I'm toying with the idea of getting a contractor's license," Mark says, "and building pools."

Earnings

The amount of money you'll make from your service depends upon the region of the country in which you work, and the length of the swimming season. Though no recent national survey has been conducted, experts in the business estimate that an experienced pool service owner can average $40,000 to $50,000 a year. However, when you're just starting in your business and building a clientele, or if you're working in an area of the country that allows for only a few summer months of swimming season, you may make less than $20,000.

Work Environment

You'll generally work alone and will probably have little client contact. Regular swimming pool servicing is not particularly strenuous, though you will be kneeling and bending, and also carrying your own equipment from your van to the pool. While you may work both indoors and outdoors, you'll usually work in pleasant weather. You'll be handling some chemicals, which may require wearing protective gloves, and possibly a mask if you're sensitive to fumes.

Pool servicing can be an excellent job for those who enjoy spending time outside. "I find cleaning pools to be kind of relaxing," Mark says, "and a good time to enjoy my surroundings. Some people find it boring and monotonous. I guess you just need a good perspective."

Outlook

Over 200,000 new pools are built every year, and this number will likely increase. With the growing number of pools, there's also growing concern for pool safety. New pool laws will be beneficial to your pool service, as you'll be hired to help pool owners meet regulations. New kinds of equipment, such as solar heaters, automatic timers, pool covers, and chemical dispensers, will keep pool services in demand. Health organizations and publications will also keep pool owners aware of the necessity of pool and hot tub cleaning to prevent infection.

For More Information

To learn more about certification, contact:

Independent Pool and Spa Service Association
17715 Chatsworth Street, Suite 203
Granada Hills, CA 91344
Tel: 818-360-9505
Web: http://www.ipssa.com

To read about issues affecting the swimming pool industry, visit the Aqua
Magazine Web page, or contact them for subscription information.

Aqua Magazine
2062 Business Center Drive
Irvine, CA 92612
Tel: 714-253-8725
Web: http://www.aquamagazine.com

Wedding/Party Planners

	School Subjects
Family and consumer science Music Theater/Dance	
	Personal Skills
Communication/ideas Leadership/management	
	Work Environment
Primarily multiple locations Indoors and Outdoors	
	Minimum Education Level
High school diploma	
	Salary Range
$22,000 to $50,000 to $100,000+	
	Certification or Licensing
Recommended	
	Outlook
Faster than the average	

Overview

From directing the bride to the best dress shops and cake decorators to pinning on the corsages the day of the wedding, *wedding/party consultants,* sometimes called *event professionals,* assist in the planning of weddings, receptions, and other large celebrations and events. These consultants generally have home-based businesses, but spend a great deal of time visiting vendors and reception and wedding sites.

History

Weddings have long provided good careers for musicians, photographers, florists, printers, caterers, and others. Even marriage "brokers" were once considered prominent members of some cultures—men and women who made their livings pairing up brides with grooms for nicely "arranged" marriages. Wedding consulting, however, has only emerged in recent years. In the years before wedding consultants, brides divided up responsibilities among cousins and aunts—a family got together to lick invitation envelopes factory-line style, a favorite aunt mixed batches of butter mints, a married sister with some recent wedding experience helped the bride pick a dress and china pattern. But usually it wasn't until after the event that the bride really had a sense of how to plan a wedding. Enter the first serious wedding consultants in the early 1980s. Recognizing how a bride can benefit a great deal from a knowledgeable guide, men and women hired themselves out as wedding and party experts. But it's only been the last few years that the major wedding magazines and publications have given serious consideration to wedding consultants. Now most wedding experts, even Martha Stewart, consider a consultant a necessity in planning a perfect and cost-efficient wedding.

The Job

Can't decide whether to have butterflies or doves released at your wedding? Want to get married on a boat, but don't know how to arrange it? Want a chef who will prepare your reception dinner table-side? Even if your requests run a little more mainstream than these, it can be difficult choosing reliable florists and other vendors, and staying within a budget. The average wedding costs close to $20,000 (including the dress), but many brides end up frustrated and disappointed with their ceremonies. Wedding consultants help brides save money and avoid stress by offering their services at the earliest stages of planning. They provide the bride with cost estimates, arrange for ceremony and reception sites, order invitations, and help select music. They also offer advice on wedding etiquette and tradition. Consultants then stay on call for their brides right through the ceremonies and receptions, pinning on flowers, instructing ushers and other members of the wedding parties, taking gifts from guests, and organizing the cake-cutting and bouquet toss.

When brides and their families seek out the services of Packy Boukis, owner of Only You Wedding and Event Consulting, she offers them "The Love Story," a full-service package of planning and organization. "I create a binder for the bride," Packy explains. "It includes a wedding schedule, the wedding party, a section for each vendor, a budget. Everything she'll need is in that book, and it's updated every four to six weeks." In these cases, Packy helps the bride with every step of the planning. She goes with the bride to visit each vendor, such as florists and photographers, to offer her advice and negotiate prices. Packy is also present at the rehearsal and the wedding to organize and see to the last-minute details, assisting in everything from floral arrangement to sewing on popped buttons. Packy has a full office in her home and works alone, with the exception of the wedding day when she has the assistance of a small staff and her husband. "My husband meets with the groomsmen," Packy says, "and makes sure the tuxes are okay."

Despite her involvement in the many different stages of a wedding's plan, Packy is quick to point out that each wedding is still very much the bride's own. "I show her three different vendors for each category," she says. "I don't dictate; it's her choice." It is Packy's responsibility as consultant to make sure that the bride has a stress-free event, and to help the bride save money. Packy benefits from discounts on services, and accepts no commissions or rebates, therefore passing savings on to the brides.

In addition to full-service consulting, Packy offers smaller, less-expensive packages. The "First Date" package is simply a single consultation, while the "I Do, I Do" package includes only wedding day assistance with the plans the bride has already made herself. Packy has also formed a place for herself on the Internet, answering wedding-related questions on "Cleveland Live" (http://forums.cleveland.com/forums/get/wedding.html), in addition to hosting a wedding consultants chat on AOL, as ITWNPacky.

Though Packy will sell invitations from time to time, she doesn't market products. Some consultants, however, sell a variety of things from candles and linens to hand-calligraphed invitations to party favors. A consultant may even own a complete bridal boutique. Some consultants specialize in only "destination" weddings. They set up services in exotic locales, like Hawaii, and handle all the details for an out-of-town bride who will only be arriving the week of the wedding. Consultants also arrange for special wedding sites like historic homes, public gardens, and resorts.

A consultant can also introduce a bride to a number of "extras" that she may not have been aware of before. In addition to arranging for the flowers, candles, and cakes, a consultant may arrange for horse-and-carriage rides, doves to be released after the ceremony, wine bars for the reception, goldfish in bowls at the tables, and other frills. Some brides rely on consultants to meet difficult requests, such as booking special kinds of musicians, or finding alternatives to flowers. Weddings on TV and in the movies often inspire brides; a candlelit wedding on "Friends" in a condemned, half-demolished church sent wedding consultants scurrying to recreate the site in their own cities.

Requirements

High School

To be a wedding consultant, you have to know about more than wedding traditions and etiquette. Above all, wedding consulting is a business, so take courses in accounting and business management. A bride will be relying on you to stay well within her budget, so you'll need to be able to balance a checkbook and work with figures. A sense of style is also very important in advising a bride on colors, flowers, and decorations—take art courses, and courses in design. A home economics course may offer lessons in floral arrangement, menu planning, fashion, tailoring, and other subjects of use to a wedding planner.

Practically any school organization will offer you a lot of experience in leadership and planning. Also, join your prom and homecoming committees, and various school fundraising events. You'll develop budgeting skills, while also learning about booking bands, photographers, and other vendors.

Postsecondary Training

A good liberal arts education can be valuable to a wedding consultant, but isn't necessary. Community college courses in small business operation can help you learn about marketing and bookkeeping. Some colleges offer courses in event planning. Courses in art and floral design are valuable, and you should take computer courses to learn how to use databases and graphics programs. Your best experience is going to be gained by actually planning weddings, which may not happen until after you've received some referrals from a professional organization. Various professional organizations offer home study programs, conferences, and seminars for wedding consultants. You should speak to representatives of the organizations to learn more about their programs, and to determine which one would be best for you. June Wedding, Inc., offers a training course available through the mail and at two community colleges. The Association of Bridal Consultants (ABC) has an apprenticeship program which links new members with established consultants. ABC also offers their Professional Development Program, a home-study program including courses in etiquette, marketing, and planning. The Association of Certified Professional Wedding Consultants has its own training program which addresses such topics as starting a business, and dealing with contracts and fees.

Certification or Licensing

Certification isn't required to work as a consultant, but it can help you build your business quickly. Packy received certification from June Wedding, Inc., an organization which also got her her first clients. Brides often contact professional associations directly, and the associations refer the brides to certified consultants in their area. Upon completing any of the training programs mentioned above, you'll receive some form of certification. Higher levels of certification exist for those who have been certified longer.

Other Requirements

From parties to vacations, Packy loves to organize things. "You should be creative," Packy advises, "and like to help people." Good people skills are very important—much of your success will rely on your relationships with vendors, musicians, and all the others you'll be hiring for weddings, as well as good word-of-mouth from previous clients. You should be good at helping people make decisions; moving clients in the right direction will be a very important part of your job. Patience is necessary, as you'll need to create a stress-free environment for the bride.

Exploring

Modern Bride, and other bridal magazines, publish many articles on wedding planning, traditions, and trends. Subscribe to a bridal magazine to get a sense of all the ins-and-outs of wedding consulting. Visit the Web sites of professional associations, as well as posting sites like Packy's at "Cleveland Live." Sites featuring questions and answers from professionals can give you a lot of insight into the business. A few cable networks feature series on weddings: "Wedding Story" on The Learning Channel depicts wedding planning documentary style; "Weddings of a Lifetime" on Lifetime Television broadcast the fantasy weddings of chosen couples.

For more hands-on experience, contact the professional organizations for the names of consultants in your area and pay them a visit. Some consultants hire assistants occasionally to help with large weddings. A part-time job with a florist, caterer, or photographer can also give you a lot of experience in wedding planning.

Employers

Most consultants are self-employed. In addition to working for brides and other individuals planning large celebrations, consultants hire on with museums and other non-profit organizations to plan fundraising events. They also work for retail stores to plan sales events, and plan grand-opening events for new businesses. Hotels, resorts, and restaurants that host a number of weddings sometimes hire consultants in full-time staff positions. Large retail stores also hire their own full-time events coordinators.

Consultants work all across the country, but are most successful in large cities. In an urban area, a consultant may be able to fill every weekend with at least one wedding. Consultants for "destination" weddings settle in popular vacation and wedding spots such as Hawaii, the Bahamas, and Las Vegas.

Starting Out

Packy worked for several years in other businesses before finding her way to self-employment. "But all my jobs," she says, "led naturally to consulting." Early on, she worked in her family's chocolate company, Mageros Candies, which gave her a strong entrepreneurial background. She holds an associate degree in business administration, and has worked as an executive secretary, and as a teacher. It was demonstrating magnetic windows for Sears that helped her develop valuable sales, presentation, and people skills. She has also worked for a bridal registry in a department store.

Many people find their way to wedding consulting after careers as events coordinators and planners, or after working weddings as caterers, florists, and musicians. If you have already developed relationships with area vendors and others involved in the planning of weddings, you may be able to start your own business without the aid of a professional organization. But if you're new to the business, it's best to go through a training program for certification. Not only will you receive instruction and professional advice, but you'll receive referrals from the organization.

With guidance, training, and a clear understanding of the responsibilities of the job, a wedding consultant can command a good fee from the onset of a new business. Start-up costs are relatively low, since you can easily work from your home with a computer, an extra phone line, and some advertising. You might want to invest in some basic software to maintain a database, to make attractive graphics for presentation purposes, and to access the Internet. Formal and semi-formal dress wear is also important, as you'll be attending many different kinds of weddings.

Advancement

As you gain experience as a consultant, you'll be able to expand your business and clientele. You'll develop relationships with area vendors that will result in more referrals and better discounts. With a bigger business, you can hire regular staff members to help you with planning, running errands, and administrative duties. Some consultants expand their services to include such perks as hand-calligraphed invitations and specially designed favors for receptions. Many consultants maintain Web sites to promote their businesses and provide wedding advice. Packy has already expanded her expertise to the World Wide Web and other media, providing interviews for *Modern Bride Magazine* and *The Wall Street Journal*. She would like to someday put together a packet of informative books for brides.

Earnings

Due to the fairly recent development of wedding consulting as a career, there haven't been any comprehensive salary surveys. Also, the number of uncertified consultants, and consultants who only plan weddings part-time, makes it difficult to estimate average earnings. Though consultants make between 10 to 15 percent of a wedding's expense, consultants generally charge a flat rate. Robbi Ernst, founder of June Wedding, Inc., has maintained a survey of consulting fees over the last 14 years. He places initial consultation fees at $275 to $425 per session, with a session lasting about three hours. A consultant may also be hired to oversee all the pre-wedding administrative details for between $1,000 and $2,000. A consultant who works the wedding day only will charge between $1,200 and $1,800. For a complete package, with assistance in the months before the wedding and up through the reception, a consultant will charge $3,000 or more. "These fees are based on educated and trained wedding consultants," Robbi says. "Our survey finds that people who have formally trained and certified can get these fees from the onset of their business if they are professional and know what they're doing."

These fees are based on consultants in metropolitan areas with populations of 500,000 or more. In a large city, an experienced consultant can realistically expect to have a wedding planned for every weekend. Because destination weddings are usually much smaller than traditional weddings, consulting fees are lower.

Work Environment

For someone who loves weddings and meeting new people, consulting can be an ideal career. Your clients may be stressed out occasionally, but most of the time they're going to be enthusiastic about planning their weddings. During the week, your hours will be spent meeting with vendors, taking phone calls, and working at the computer. Your weekends will be a bit faster paced, among larger crowds, and you'll get to see the results of your hard work—you'll be at the wedding sites, fussing over final details and making sure everything goes smoothly.

Your office hours won't be affected by weather conditions, but on the actual wedding days you'll be expected to get easily and quickly from one place to the other. Bad weather on the day of an outdoor wedding can result in more work for you as you move everything to the "rain site." One of the perks of wedding consulting is taking an active part in someone's celebration; part of your job is making sure everyone has a good time. But you'll also be expected to be present for weddings, receptions, and rehearsal dinners, which means you'll be working weekends and occasional evenings.

Outlook

There are currently four professional organizations devoted to furthering the careers of wedding consultants. This will result in more awareness of the career in the public, and therefore a more cautious clientele. Uncertified consultants will find it increasingly difficult to find work. With this increased career awareness, more community colleges will offer courses in wedding and event planning.

According to Robbi Ernst of June Wedding, Inc., the people getting married for the first time are older, better educated, and more sophisticated. They're paying for their own weddings and have more original ideas for their ceremonies. Also, more people are celebrating their anniversaries by renewing their vows with large events. Wedding consultants will want to capitalize on this trend, as well as expand into other ceremonies like bar and bat mitzvahs.

Wedding consulting is one of few career fields which will not likely be affected much by technology. Though fads and trends do change weddings slightly from season to season, wedding ceremonies are based on old traditions. Most brides like to adhere to wedding etiquette, and to have weddings similar to those they imagined as children. Desktop publishing may change the consultant's office somewhat, resulting in some consultants designing their own invitations. Consultants may even expand their areas by assisting brides over the Internet.

For More Information

Either visit the June Wedding Web site for training and certification information, or send a check for $15, along with a letter requesting information, to the following address:

June Wedding, Inc. (An Association for Event Professionals)
1331 Burnham Avenue
Las Vegas, NV 89104-3658
Tel: 792-474-9558
Web: http://www.junewedding.com

For information on home-study and professional designations, contact:

Association of Bridal Consultants
200 Chestnut Land Road
New Milford, CT 06776-2521
Tel: 860-355-0464
Web: http://www.trainingforum.com/ASN/ABC/index.html

For information on training programs, home-study, and certification, contact:

National Bridal Service
3122 West Cary Street
Richmond, VA 23221
Tel: 804-355-6945
Web: http://www.nationalbridalservice.com

For information on training programs, contact:

Association of Certified Professional Wedding Consultants
7791 Prestwick Circle
San Jose, CA 95135
Tel: 408-528-9000
Web: http://www.acpwc.com/

Index

Franchise Owners

	School Subjects
Business Mathematics	
	Personal Skills
Following instructions Leadership/management	
	Work Environment
Primarily one location Primarily indoors	
	Minimum Education Level
High school diploma	
	Salary Range
$25,000 to $87,000 to $171,000+	
	Certification or Licensing
None available	
	Outlook
Faster than the average	

Overview

A *franchise owner* contracts with a company to sell the company's products or services. After paying an initial fee, and agreeing to pay the company a certain percentage of revenue, the franchise owner can use the company's name, logo, and guidance. McDonald's, Subway, and Dairy Queen are some of the top franchise opportunities; these companies have franchises all across the country. Franchises account for over 80 billion dollars in annual sales in the United States, and 40 percent of all U.S. retail sales.

History

Know anybody with an antique Singer sewing machine? Chances are, it was originally sold by one of the first franchise operations. During the Civil War, the Singer Sewing Machine Company recognized the cost-efficiency of franchising, and allowed dealers across the country to sell its sewing machines. Coca-Cola, as well as the Ford Motor Company and other automobile manufacturers, followed Singer's lead in the early 20th century by granting indi-